The Question Of Jesus

ISBN 0 7151 0434 9
Published for the General Synod Board of Education
by Church House Publishing 1987

Designed and produced by The Creative House, Saffron Walden, Essex.
Cover by Clare Holland.

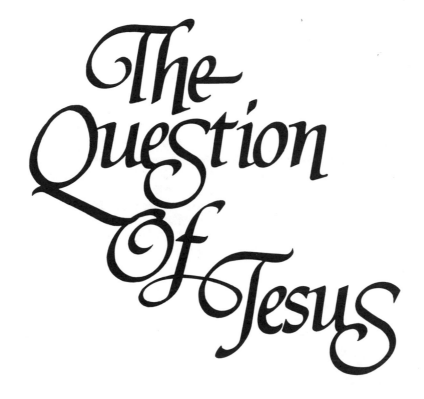

The Question Of Jesus

by
Colin Alves, Alan T. Dale and Christopher Herbert

With a Foreword by the Rt Rev. John Austin Baker,
Bishop of Salisbury

CHURCH HOUSE PUBLISHING
Church House, Great Smith Street, London SW1P 3NZ

About the pictures in this book

These are NOT meant as illustrations to the different chapters. They are photographs of works of art from Roman times to the present day which show how people have thought of Jesus at different times and in different ways. They are included to help you think about the question 'How do I see Jesus?' You might like to choose which one you like best, and to decide why; to consider what the artists were trying to express; or to look elsewhere and find some other pictures which appeal more to you personally. There are notes about the photographs at the back of the book.

Contents

Foreword

by the Bishop of Salisbury, the Rt Rev. John Austin Baker

The idea for *The Question of Jesus* began in 1976. That great Christian and teacher, Alan T. Dale, who had done so much to make the Bible come alive for young people and all engaged in Religious Education, was concerned that so much of the material being produced for schools seemed to take little account of all the positive work of modern scholars who have done so much to deepen and enliven our understanding of the Old and New Testaments.

There seemed to be something of an anxiety in some publishing circles that material about the Bible must play safe, and make only statements that no one, whatever their religious viewpoint, could object to. Alan felt that the bland and unbelievable results of that kind of caution were making Christianity itself unbelievable to youngsters who were well informed in school on other subjects, and encouraged to be critical. Only RE offered them a 2-D world. We needed to give it 3-D flesh-and-blood reality.

He suggested starting right at the heart of the matter with a book about Jesus — a book which would boldly make use of our vastly increased knowledge of the world of Jesus and our new ideas about the way the Gospels were written. Thanks to the generosity of the Wadderton Trust a working group was set up, consisting of Alan himself, Colin Alves, Christopher Herbert and Pamela Egan. I was invited to take on the exciting task of theological consultant, and gladly accepted. We used to meet regularly at the Worcester diocesan retreat and conference house at Cropthorne, and exhausting but enthusiastic meetings they were.

In January 1979, tragically, Alan died, leaving a first draft of the first part of the book. Quite apart from missing his amazing gifts of style in writing for teenagers, we all felt a deep sense of personal bereavement, so much had he inspired us with his vision and friendship. If this book has any virtues, we would all like to think of them as our posthumous tribute of love and admiration to him.

Colin Alves and Christopher Herbert have completed the task in the sparse intervals they have been able to snatch from crowded professional lives, and I believe they have done a marvellous job, producing a book which should help teachers to impart a wholly new quality to their teaching about Jesus of Nazareth.

The need which Alan Dale discerned is still very much with us. Experience with teaching the Bible to very varied groups has convinced me that modern scholarship, imaginatively used, makes the Scriptures – and especially the Gospels – a hundred times more real and interesting. To deny our secondary school pupils this advantage is stupid and wrong. May this book give new confidence to those who teach and inspiration to those who learn, and set a new standard in this particular area of religious education.

+ JOHN SARUM

PART I

'The Good Shepherd' (Roman, about 330 AD)

Introduction

Two thousand years ago a child was born who changed the world. The facts of his life, as far as we know them, are simple and few. He grew up in a small town, Nazareth, in Galilee, an area of Palestine ruled over by the forces of an occupying power, the Romans. His mother was called Mary and his father Joseph, and he was the eldest of a large family. When he was about thirty years old he left his home, gave up his job, and became a wandering teacher, story-teller and healer. A number of people became his followers, including twelve men whom he called his disciples. But his teaching and way of life outraged some of his fellow-countrymen and eventually they had him arrested, flogged and executed. His friends claimed that he rose from the dead and that he was God's Son. That is the bare outline of the life of the man, Jesus.

Two thousand years later there are 900 million people throughout the world, in every country, of every race and colour, who claim to be his followers. Clearly a man who has had such an astonishing influence upon the world must be worth learning more about and the claims his followers make for him must be worth studying.

'Christ the Ruler of All' (Mosaic from Ravenna, about 1100 AD)

1

The world that Jesus lived in

Everybody is influenced by the people with whom they live and by the country in which they grow up. Jesus is no exception and in order to begin to understand him we need to take a brief look at his background.

In many ways Jesus' world was very like ours. It was a world of people like ourselves who had to learn to live together and get on with each other.

They had the same range of abilities that we have. They knew about friendship and loyalty and being let down. They knew hunger, poverty and plenty. They knew about injustice and power and the schemes of politicians. They knew about the strains and stresses of family life, and they knew happy times when whole villages were alive with the sound of dancing and singing and laughter. But it was also a turbulent, restless and dangerously frightened world in which they lived.

The area of land known as Palestine had been invaded by the Romans in 63 BC, and there followed an uneasy truce between the conquerors' army and the occupied peoples, which was punctuated by outbreaks of guerilla warfare and terrorism. The Romans established a puppet-king, Herod, who ruled from 37 BC to 4 BC and was then succeeded by three of his sons (Archelaus, Herod Antipas and Philip). The territory over which he had ruled was divided into three with each of them in charge of a particular area. The Romans found Herod a useful and trustworthy king, for he was a champion of law and order. The Jews called him, sarcastically, 'half Jew' and thought of him as a pagan tyrant willing to harm his people if it would promote his own cause. Two of his three sons were little different. Archelaus remained a ruler for only ten years and he was then sent into exile by the Romans. Herod Antipas was clever and ambitious and in fact lasted for forty-three years, but eventually was exiled. Philip (4 BC – AD 34) by contrast was praised for the goodness of his rule. At his death in AD 34 the territory was given first to the Roman province of Syria and then back to Herod's grandson Agrippa.

As you may imagine, it was a fairly fragile political situation for a people who for centuries had seen their land as given to them by God and who regarded trespassers upon their territory with angry contempt.

Jesus himself would have been only too aware of the dangerous times in which he was living. Just over the hills from Nazareth lay a town called Sepphoris. From that town Judas of Gamala had tried to organise an armed revolt against the Romans in AD 6. It was a horrifying failure. A Roman general called Varus moved in to crush it. He smashed the town to the ground, setting fire to the buildings, and then, as a grim warning to the people, crucified the rebels on crosses at the roadside.

As is often the case the suppression only served to create what we would now call an underground resistance. A movement whose members were known as the *Zealots* was born out of the smouldering ashes of Sepphoris. Intensely religious, they were fanatically opposed to their holy land being in the hands of heathen foreigners and carried out acts of violence and terrorism. They were called by various names, sometimes *'sicarii'* (a *sicarius* was a short dagger); and sometimes simply 'robbers' or 'brigands'. They saw their task as a clean-cut affair. It was to kill as many Romans as possible and to murder any Jews who dared to collaborate. Some of Jesus' closest friends and disciples may well have been members of that guerilla movement; indeed, one of them was called Simon the Zealot.

It would be false, however, to suggest that the entire population of the country was in a state of excitable resentment. There were some who saw the Roman occupation as a very acceptable thing. After all, it brought law (no matter how harsh), roads and trade. For those so inclined the occupation could be turned to profit. In this category you could place a group known as the *Sadducees.* They were a powerful, aristocratic elite who generally provided the high priests and the elders of the nation. Not as fanatically religious as the Zealots, they were willing to temper their beliefs in the light of the political situation.

If the Sadducees worked with the Romans and saw life as a matter of political survival, the *Essenes* decided that holy withdrawal was the only answer. We have learnt a great deal more about this group over the past forty years, following the discovery of some of their writings at a deserted valley called Qumran, near the Dead Sea. They had decided to retreat into the more barren regions of the country to purify themselves in readiness for what they saw as the day of God's coming. In common with many of their fellow Jews they believed that God was active in world events. They believed that God, centuries before, had guided their ancestors from Egypt to Israel. They believed that he spoke directly to the prophets and kings of old and that he was constantly interfering in history to ensure the survival of his Chosen People. God, they thought, would come to earth, drive out the occupying Roman forces and make Israel the throne from which he would control and rule over the rest of the world.

The Essenes took these beliefs, held by many of the Jewish people, to extremes. There are some who say that John the Baptist or even Jesus himself may have spent some time with an Essene community. Whether this was so or not does not matter for the purpose of this book – but what the Essenes remind us about is the anxious, lively, sometimes fanatical zeal with which many Jews looked forward to the coming of God to earth. Even if the Essenes were only a tiny minority, as undoubtedly they were, many shared their basic belief in the imminent destruction of the world and the coming of God's Kingdom. This was a major factor contributing to the feverish and excited mood of the country.

The fourth group with whom we know Jesus had dealings, were the *Pharisees.* The word Pharisee probably means 'separatist'. They were the religious leaders of the time. They separated themselves from everything that they thought would displease God – and in particular they kept themselves separate from the common people, believing that these had no proper understanding of religion. And they kept themselves separate from 'foreigners'. They considered it utterly wrong to have a meal with such people or even to go into their houses. To do so, they believed, would make you 'unclean'. This was not from irrational prejudice but from the way they interpreted the 'Law'. As far as they were concerned the Law was God-given and in order to please God the Law had to be obeyed to the letter. The good were those who did this, the bad those who disobeyed. Although they did help the poor in society, they unfortunately became obsessed with the application of the Law to the most minor and un-important activities – and became very strict in their judgements.

A society as volatile and as fragmented as Palestine was during the lifetime of Jesus needed something firm and strong to hold it all together. At the heart of it was, of course, the Jewish religion intertwined with the social customs of the day and it is to this that we now turn.

2

The religious beliefs of the time

The Jewish people did not divide up their activities into compartments as we do. They thought of all human activity as one – politics and work and the worship of God in the synagogue were simply different ways of being religious. Their customs were 'religious' customs; the justification for them could be found in the Bible scrolls. The war against the Romans for which the Zealots were preparing was a 'religious' war – a 'Holy war'. Everything that there was had 'religious' overtones.

It is this way of looking at things that marked the Jews off from other people. They saw themselves as 'God's People'. Their state was a religious community. Their leaders were religious leaders. Their teachers were religious teachers. Their schools took place in the synagogue and the students studied the Bible scrolls.

But what did these people believe about God? Luke tells a story about Jesus in the synagogue of his home town of Nazareth which will help to highlight their beliefs. Here is the story.

Jesus went to Nazareth, where he had been brought up and on the Sabbath day he went as usual to the synagogue. He stood up to read the scriptures and was handed the book of the prophet Isaiah. He unrolled the scroll and found the place where it is written,
'The Spirit of the Lord is upon me,
because he has chosen me to bring good news to the poor.
He has sent me to proclaim liberty to the captives and recovery of sight to the blind;
to set free the oppressed and announce that the time has come
when the Lord will save his people.'

(Luke 4.16–19)

It is worth noting that here Jesus was sharing in the worship of his village with the people he had known since childhood. They were meeting in the synagogue, the central religious meeting place of the village, in which the scrolls of the Law were kept and given a special and honoured position. Jesus would have been with the men and the older boys in the part of the synagogue reserved for them, whilst the women, the girls and the younger boys looked on.

The synagogues had only become important in the life of the Jewish people following their arrival back in Palestine in 587 BC after a long exile in Babylonia. They had become places of worship and study, but they did not supplant the special role of the Temple. This was the central and most holy of all Jewish religious buildings and had been built in Jerusalem. It was considered the duty of every Jew to go to the Temple at least once in his lifetime. There he would have seen a beautiful and richly ornamented series of buildings, crowded with animals being led to the slaughter. In the centre of the Temple was the most sacred place of all. It was called 'The Holy of Holies'. Only the High Priest was allowed to enter this place, a small windowless cube containing the Ark which was thought of as God's throne.

They considered God as a remote and awe-ful being, the Creator of all things; all-powerful and all-just. His ways were unsearchable, but he governed all according to his law, which was valid for eternity. Everything that happened, happened according to his fore-knowledge and things were moving inevitably towards their final fulfilment. But above all else God was the God of Israel, of the Jewish people. He had chosen them centuries before as a special people, revealing to them, through Abraham, Moses and the prophets, his laws and commandments. Even though God was seen as righteous and just, some Jews admitted to finding it difficult to understand why he let some things happen as they did. Some believed in a life after death where everything would be sorted out justly. Not only was God seen as Judge, however; he was also seen to be caring. His steadfast love could be trusted and it 'endured for ever'. He cared for his people as a father cares for his family. Jesus would have learnt much of this in the very synagogue where he was now preaching.

But how does it work out in reality? What do these beliefs actually mean in the day to day life of a village or of the country as a whole? This is where Jesus began to find difficulties.

Perhaps we might summarise those difficulties by saying that his countrymen believed that God was first and foremost a law-giver and secondly that his main concern was with his chosen people, the Jews. The laws of God, though meant for everybody, were to be found only in the Torah (the first five books of the Bible), and only the Jewish people tried to keep them. God was the God of the whole world, but the world outside the Jews was 'heathen'. There were many sincere Jews who cared that the world should really be God's world and its people truly worship him. But the only way they could think that this might be achieved was by all the foreigners becoming Jews. This meant not only changing their religion but changing their nationality too. On both these points Jesus took a different line.

We can see this if we look further at the account of that synagogue service. Note the passage from the Bible scroll which Jesus read. It was not the passage which contains the ten commandments. It was a passage where the prophet is describing his work, and his work was concerned with the poor, prisoners, blind people, conquered people, all people in need. The congregation would have no quarrel with this nor with Jesus' statement that this was happening now in their own time. Many people believed that God would soon be coming to deliver their world from all its sorrows. Up to this point Pharisees and freedom-fighters (i.e. Zealots) too would agree. But the words had a deeper and wider meaning than they understood. This became clear when Jesus went on to say what the words meant to him.

He took two stories from the Bible scroll that everybody knew, but they were both about foreigners, a foreign widow and a foreign soldier. The point, Jesus was saying, was that God cared equally for everybody, for foreigners as well as Jews. Immediately the synagogue was in uproar. He had touched on a deeply felt issue – the national pride of the Jews.

10

But Jesus probably chose the passage from the Bible scroll for an even deeper reason. What mattered was not keeping the laws, but caring for people, caring for the prisoners, the blind and the poor. And real caring does not make any distinction between people. If people are in need then those needs must be met, regardless of colour, creed, nationality or sex. He even pushed this teaching to the limits, saying that men should not only care for people they liked but their love should extend to their enemies as well.

'Love your enemies, do good to those who hate you, bless those who curse you and pray for those who illtreat you. If anyone hits you on one cheek, let him hit the other one too; if someone takes your coat, let him have your shirt as well. Give to everyone who asks you for something, and when someone takes what is yours, do not ask for it back. Do for others just what you want them to do for you.'

(Luke 6.27–31)

You can perhaps see now why Jesus, believing in a God who cared for all alike, should have behaved in the way he did. If God loved everyone, then men should do the same. Jesus expressed these beliefs in a practical and astonishing fashion.

Once Jesus was in a certain town where there was a man who was suffering from a dreaded skin disease. When he saw Jesus, he threw himself down and begged him,
'Sir, if you want to, you can make me clean!'
Jesus stretched out his hand and touched him.
'I do want to,' he answered. 'Be clean!' At once the disease left the man.   (Luke 5.12–13)

It was not just the poor and the despised whom Jesus touched.
Some people brought children to Jesus for him to place his hands on them, but the disciples scolded the people. When Jesus noticed this he was angry and said to his disciples: 'Let the children come to me, and do not stop them, because the kingdom of God belongs to such as these. I assure you that whoever does not receive the kingdom of God like a child will never enter it.' Then he took the children in his arms, placed his hands on each of them and blessed them.

(Mark 10.13–16)

The claims that Jesus made about God, he lived out in his own life, but those were the very claims which outraged some of his countrymen. In Nazareth they even tried to lynch him.

In the face of such bitter opposition, how did Jesus find the strength to carry on? No doubt he was sustained by his profound and fundamental beliefs about God. They were beliefs so deep and so central to his being that they were more like knowledge than 'beliefs'. He seemed to know that his vision of God was the true vision. It could all be summed up in the way he prayed to God in his own prayers. He began his prayers by saying 'Abba' (Father). The word he used was not the dignified word to be found in the synagogue prayers; it was the familiar and endearing name for 'father' used in the home, more like the world 'Dad' than anything else. God was as close and as caring and as involved as that.

Then Jesus said to the disciples, 'And so I tell you not to worry about the food you need to stay alive, or about the clothes you need for your body. Life is much more important than food, and the body much more important than clothes . . . Your Father knows that you need these things. Instead, be concerned with his Kingdom, and he will provide you with these things.'

(Luke 12.22–23, 30–31)

For the Jews, God was creator and law-giver and judge. For Jesus, he was all these, but much, much more. He was 'Father' – father of all men, and he wanted mankind to share with him in his work of love.

3

The central message of Jesus

The religious leaders, the freedom-fighters and even the common people must have found Jesus a puzzle. He said and did many things with which they could whole-heartedly agree – their own rabbis had said and done as much, they would say. But it was the way he did things and the way he said things which upset them. It was good to heal people, as one synagogue leader said, but why do it on the Sabbath? God is Father, but why must it be that he cares for everybody? It all looked too much like a deliberate attack upon the deeply-held beliefs of his countrymen.

But Jesus was not so much attacking the religion of his people as calling them back to what that religion was all about, to what God was really like.

What Jesus stood for could really be put quite simply: religion was not about rules and regulations, it was about how you lived. If rules and regulations stood in the way of living a good life, then get rid of them. And what was a 'good life'? 'If anybody wants to know what a good life is,' Jesus would have said, 'it is easy. It is living in God's way and God's way is the way of caring.'

We can see what Jesus himself understood by living in God's way if we examine a fairly typical day in his life. As it happens Mark's gospel opens with such a description, both of what Jesus said and what he stood for.

The day Mark describes begins at about ten o'clock in the morning and goes on to just after dawn the next day. He may have heard Peter talk about what a day with Jesus was like; his account of the day certainly reads as if it were the report of an eye-witness. Here it is:

> Jesus and his disciples came to the town of Capernaum and on the next Sabbath Jesus went into the synagogue and began to teach. The people who heard him were amazed at the way he taught, for he wasn't like the teachers of the Law; instead, he taught with authority.
>
> Just then a man with an evil spirit in him came into the Synagogue and screamed, 'What do you want with us, Jesus of Nazareth? Are you here to destroy us? I know who you are – you are God's holy messenger!'

Jesus ordered the spirit, 'Be quiet and come out of the man!' The evil spirit shook the man hard, gave a loud scream, and came out of him. The people were all so amazed that they started saying to one another, 'What is this? Is it some kind of new teaching? This man has authority to give orders to the evil spirits and they obey him!' And so the news about Jesus spread quickly everywhere in the province of Galilee.

Jesus and his disciples, including James and John, left the synagogue, and went straight to the home of Simon and Andrew. Simon's mother-in-law was sick in bed with a fever, and as soon as Jesus arrived, he was told about her. He went to her, took her by the hand, and helped her up. The fever left her, and she began to wait on them.

After the sun had set and evening had come, people brought to Jesus all the sick and those who had demons. All the people of the town gathered in front of the house. Jesus healed many who were sick with all kinds of diseases and drove out many demons. He would not let the demons say anything, because they knew who he was.

Very early the next morning, long before daylight, Jesus got up and left the house. He went out of the town to a lonely place, where he prayed. But Simon and his companions went out searching for him, and when they found him, they said, 'Everyone is looking for you.'

But Jesus answered, 'We must go on to the other villages round here. I have to preach in them also, because that is why I came.'

(Mark 1.21–39)

This is a lively picture of what Jesus was doing and saying, but note that at the end of the day, he went off to a lonely place to pray. That is, he found somewhere very quiet where he could think things through in the presence of God. It could well be that he was troubled by the reception the people were giving him. They were treating him as a travelling doctor and not really listening to the 'good news' about God which he had to bring.

So let us now compare this story with what the 'good news' was. All Jesus had to say, Mark tells us, could be summed up in these four phrases:

The Great Day is here.
God's kingdom has come.
Change your ways,
and trust in the good news.

(Mark 1.15)

The first two statements are about God and they are astonishing in their claims. 'The "Great Day" is not a far off event, says Jesus, 'it has arrived. It is a present experience which men and women can share here and now.' 'More than that, though,' says Jesus, 'God is not a remote absentee landlord, he is in charge here and now.' You may imagine the way these two claims would puzzle people. Surely the coming of God would be more dramatic? Surely there would be some signs of power and triumph? And as for God's being in charge – where could he be seen? Where was the evidence?

Jesus' teaching was not only a statement about God's rule having begun; it was also a call to men to change their ways. If God's power, God's rule was to be part and parcel of their daily lives they had to change (repent) and trust God, for the good news is good news about God.

14

Let us look more closely at the words Mark has used here to describe what Jesus had to say.

The 'Great Day' or 'God's Day' is an old phrase. It goes back to the earliest times of the Jewish people. In those very early days God was thought of by the Hebrew tribes as the 'God of Battles' ('Lord of Hosts' is the phrase you sometimes see). He was their leader in war, their great supernatural and powerful warrior. (Many early peoples thought of their gods in the same way.) Their wars, therefore, were 'holy wars'. The freedom-fighters of the Galilee used these old stories to prove they were right to call the men of their own day to another, the last, 'Holy War'. But the Hebrew prophets had had no use for this way of thinking about God's Day. For them 'God's Day' had meant the triumph of God's *good* purposes; it had nothing to do with any kind of narrow patriotism. God's Day would be a very different kind of day from what many people looked forward to. This is how the prophet Amos could speak about it.

How terrible it will be for you who long for the day of the Lord! What good will that day do you? For you it will be a day of darkness and not of light. It will be like a man who runs from a lion and meets a bear! Or like a man who comes home and puts his hand on the wall – only to be bitten by a snake! The day of the Lord will bring darkness and not light; it will be a day of gloom, without any brightness.

The Lord says, 'I hate your religious festivals; I cannot stand them! When you bring me burnt-offerings and grain-offerings, I will not accept them; I will not accept the animals you have fattened to bring me as offerings. Stop your noisy songs; I do not want to listen to your harps. Instead, let justice flow like a stream, and righteousness like a river that never goes dry.'

(Amos 5.18–24)

For Amos and the other prophets that Day was in the future. Nobody knew when it would come. But for Jesus, that Day had already come. God was working then and there in their midst; his triumph over evil and wrong had begun. There was no more waiting for God to act; he was already acting in the lives of men and women.

It must be said, though, that even if Jesus proclaimed that God's Day had come, he still thought there was something that needed to be fulfilled in the future. It was as if part of the Day had dawned and the rest was yet to come.

He warned the disciples and his followers to be prepared.
'No one knows, however, when that day or hour will come – neither the angels in heaven nor the Son: only the Father knows. Be on watch, be alert, for you do not know when the time will come. It will be like a man who goes away from home on a journey and leaves his servants in charge, after giving to each one his own work to do and after telling the door-keeper to keep watch. Be on guard then, because you do not know when the master of the house is coming – it might be in the evening, or at midnight, or before dawn or at sunrise. If he comes suddenly, he must not find you asleep. What I say to you, then, I say to all: Watch!'

(Mark 13.32–37)

Jesus, then, said that God's Day had come, but it was not as people had expected. It was quieter, less dramatic, almost hidden, and there was still a future moment when God would appear in power and triumph to judge the world.

But even if the Day had not yet been completed, Jesus seemed to be saying that God's rule had begun. And what kind of rule was it? In describing the typical day, Mark seems to be showing us how Jesus understood God's rule, God's kingship, God's kingdom. It was the rule of good over evil; after all, Jesus had driven out the evil spirits. It was the rule of love, in which people who were sick and in pain could be healed; Jesus cared for the madman, for Peter's mother-in-law, for the sick people who came crowding round the door when the Holy Day ended at sunset. God's rule was not violent or terrifying; it meant caring for the poor, the mad, the overlooked. Caring so much that healing was part of the process. (We shall look at the 'problem' of the healing miracles later.)

The other part of Jesus' message was that people should repent – literally, should turn around and face the other way. They should turn around and look at God, acknowledge his rule, and then learn to live afresh by trusting in him. In Luke's gospel, following the account of Jesus teaching his disciples his own prayer, he says:

'Suppose one of you should go to a friend's house at midnight and say to him, "Friend, let me borrow three loeaves of bread. A friend of mine who is on a journey has come to my house and I haven't got any food for him!" And suppose your friend should answer from inside, "Don't bother me! The door is already locked, and my children and I are in bed. I can't get up and give you anything." Well, what then? I tell you that even if he will not get up and give you the bread because you are his friend, yet he will get up and give you everything you need because you are not ashamed to keep on asking.'

'And so I say to you: "Ask, and you will receive; seek, and you will find; knock, and the door will be opened to you . . ." Bad as you are, you know how to give good things to your children. How much more, then, will the Father in heaven give the Holy Spirit to those who ask him.'

(Luke 11.5–9, Matt. 7.11)

As in all that Jesus said and did, his teaching and preaching came out of his beliefs in and about God. From what he knew about God, he knew that God's way was the way of caring, and for people to share in that they had to be changed, and then, trusting in God, they too could share in proclaiming the 'good news'. Jesus' message was simple and in that simplicity lay its authority and power.

4

Jesus' challenge to society

The beliefs Jesus had about God led him to challenge society at its roots. In fact many of the stories about him tell of his getting into trouble because he so often did what other people thought should not be done. It was not that he did not care about customs. He did. But he asked questions about them and, when convinced that a custom was no longer good, he ignored or broke it. He ate with people regarded as outcasts, for example, something a devout Jew would have found abhorrent.

> While Jesus was having a meal in Matthew's house, many tax-collectors and other outcasts came and joined Jesus and his disciples at table. Some Pharisees saw this and asked his disciples, 'Why does your teacher eat with such people?' Jesus heard them and answered, 'People who are well do not need a doctor, but only those who are sick. Go and find out what is meant by the scripture that says: "It is kindness that I want, not animal sacrifices.' I have not come to call respectable people, but the outcasts."'
>
> (Matthew 9.10–13)

You will notice that Jesus does not break the custom simply to be different or difficult, but because he believed that scriptural teaching demanded this.

There were possibly times, though, when even Jesus seems to have had some difficulty in freeing himself from the customs of the day, not least those customs which he had assumed were correct and good. Is the following story perhaps an example of how Jesus' own understanding of things was changed?

> A woman, whose daughter had an evil spirit in her, heard about Jesus and came to him at once and fell at his feet. The woman was a Gentile, born in the region of Phoenicia in Syria. She begged Jesus to drive the demon out of her daughter. But Jesus answered, 'Let us first feed the children. It isn't right to take the children's food and throw it to the dogs.'
>
> (Mark 7.25–27)

Was Jesus indicating by this that he believed he had been sent only to care for the Jews and not anyone else? The woman's reply is a real challenge to him –

> 'Sir, even the dogs under the table eat the children's leftovers!' So Jesus said to her, 'Because of that answer, go back home, where you will find that the demon has gone out of your daughter!' She went home and found her child lying on the bed; the demon had indeed gone out of her.
>
> (Mark 7.28–30)

You can see how quickly people would begin to talk about Jesus – breaking the normally accepted social customs of his day. Eating with tax-collectors. Talking with foreign women. 'What will he get up to next?' 'What does he think he's doing?' 'It looks as though he enjoys flouting all the things which decent people stand for.' 'Doesn't he care?'

Matters became much more serious, however, when Jesus began breaking the most respected religious customs of the country. One of the most important customs (as the Law Book required) was the custom of doing no work on the Sabbath Day. Even healing people on this holy day was simply not allowed. Here is how Jesus dealt with that.

(He) went back to the synagogue, where there was a man who had a paralysed hand. Some people were there who wanted to accuse Jesus of doing wrong; so they watched him closely to see whether he would heal the man on the Sabbath. Jesus said to the man, 'Come up here to the front.' Then he asked the people 'What does our Law allow us to do on the Sabbath? To help or to harm? To save a man's life or to destroy it?'

But they did not say a thing. Jesus was angry as he looked around at them, but at the same time he felt sorry for them, because they were so stubborn and wrong. Then he said to the man, 'Stretch out your hand.' He stretched it out, and it became well again.

(Mark 3.1–5)

It was a critical moment in Jesus' life as it happens, because from then on, according to Mark's gospel, the Pharisees and some of Herod's officials met and made plans to kill him.

Jesus seemed to be concerned that the religious customs of the time should meet men's needs. If someone was ill and needed help then, Sabbath or no Sabbath, he should be helped. Or suppose someone was hungry – then he should be able to eat. When the disciples were walking through a cornfield one Sabbath day and began to pluck ears of corn to nibble, the Pharisees accused them of breaking the law, for plucking corn was considered to be work. After reminding them that king David had once broken the law to suit his purpose, Jesus replied very crisply, 'The Sabbath was made for the good of man; man was not made for the Sabbath.' (Mark 2.27)

With Jesus causing such a stir as this, it was no wonder that his family became anxious for his safety. If he got into trouble then they too might be drawn into it, so they tried to persuade him to come home.

Jesus' mother and brothers arrived. They stood outside the house and sent in a message, asking for him. A crowd was sitting around Jesus and they said to him, 'Look, your mother and brothers are outside, and they want you.'

Jesus answered, 'Who is my mother? Who are my brothers?' He looked at the people sitting round him and said, 'Look! Here are my mother and my brothers! Whoever does what God wants him to do is my brother, my sister, my mother.'   (Mark 3.31-35)

It was like throwing down the gauntlet. If Jesus were breaking the religious rules on the grounds that they were not what God required, and then said that any others who did what God wanted were his brothers and sisters, you can see what a revolutionary he was. It was as though he were undermining the very foundations of society.

And he went further than suggesting that some of these religious rules were not very important. He seems to have believed that some of them were actually the opposite of what God wanted.

Here is a clear example of this:
And Jesus continued 'You have a clever way of rejecting God's law in order to uphold your own teaching! For Moses commanded, "Respect your father and your mother" and, "Whoever curses his father or his mother must be put to death." But you teach that if a person has something he could use to help his father or mother, but says "This is Corban" (which means, it belongs to God), he is excused from helping his father or mother. In this way the teaching you pass on to others cancels out the word of God.'

(Mark 7.9–13)

But Jesus was really much more anxious to direct people's attention positively to what God wanted. He cut through all the laws and the teachings and went straight to the heart of the matter. For example, in the teaching about divorce which was then common among his countrymen, it was permissible for a man to divorce his wife, although there was some disagreement about what constituted good grounds for divorce. What seems certain about the Jewish marriage customs of the time, however, is that only the man could divorce the woman, never the other way round. These details need not detain us here. What we want to demonstrate is how Jesus referred his questioners back, not only to the laws of Moses, but to the origin of those laws: God himself.
'In the beginning, at the time of creation, "God made them male and female," as the Scripture says. "And for this reason a man will leave his father and mother and unite with his wife, and the two will become one." So they are no longer two, but one. Man must not separate, then, what God has joined together.'

(Mark 10.6–9)

Jesus seemed to be saying to his fellow countrymen – 'Look! If you want to decide how to live, don't burden yourself with all these man-made traditions. Live your life in the light of what God wants.' It was a simple, but challenging way of cutting through the thousands of legal strands which had been woven by the religious lawyers, the scribes, and it came from Jesus' deep-rooted conviction about what God was like. It was that underlying sense of purpose which gave Jesus his directness and his extraordinary power.

5

Jesus the teacher

Like anyone with a message to proclaim, like any teacher, Jesus had to work out how he could most effectively say what he wanted to say. How could he put what God had given him to say in such a way that people would have to listen and that what they heard would stick in their minds? It was a real problem, for he probably realised that, when it became quite clear what he had to say, his fellow-countrymen would refuse to listen to him any further.

He chose to use stories and poems to convey his message.

Why stories? Stories do several things. First of all, everybody likes listening to them. Secondly it is only in stories that we can really talk about God; stories can hint and suggest and mean far more than they seem to say on the surface. Thirdly, stories can be told in such a way that they raise questions and make people think. They are very different from slogans. People can shout slogans without having any idea of what the slogans mean. The freedom-fighters could shout 'The kingdom of God' or 'God is our king', but what did they mean? Jesus wanted to convey far more than slogans, he wanted to try to show people what God was like.

The stories Jesus told, and he was a wonderfully gifted story-teller, are not as simple as they look. The images or pictures he used he took from many places – things he noticed when he was a boy, stories he had heard told in the villages, incidents that had happened in his time, poems from the Bible scrolls he had read with his teacher. The stories, too, are always very carefully constructed. They move to a climax and it is the ending of the story that is important to note. Further, the stories as Jesus told them are not actually 'finished', they seem to stop just before the end and leave us saying 'But what happened then?' This is something the listener has to work out for himself. For the stories were meant to provoke questions, not answer them.

The great power of stories, though, is that we can read them on several levels. At the top-most level they are real stories about incidents which might have happened anywhere, to anybody in any village or farm, but at levels underneath they have a deeper meaning and often an unexpected twist. Jesus made it quite clear what his stories were really about by beginning them with 'The kingdom of God is like . . .'

Look at this story he once told:

'The kingdom of God is like this. A man scatters seed in his field. He sleeps at night, is up and about during the day, and all the while the seeds are sprouting and growing. Yet he does not know how it happens. The soil itself makes the plants grow and bear fruit; first the tender stalk appears, then the ear, and finally the ear full of corn. When the corn is ripe, the man starts cutting it with his sickle, because harvest time has come.'

(Mark 4.26–29)

Now notice what Jesus does. He first of all says that it is a story about God's rule. Anybody listening who sympathised with the freedom-fighters would prick up his ears at that 'slogan'. Then it continues as a brilliant picture of an ordinary farmer quietly going about his farm work, trusting the soil, going to bed at night with a quiet mind and getting up in the morning to get on with his work, until harvest time.

But there are some things to note (his Jewish listeners would spot them). The story is about a farmer and his farm; his listeners would know that in the Old Testament, a 'farm' is often used as a picture of the Jewish people. 'Ah,' says a listener. 'Isaiah used a picture of a farm to describe us; I wonder what he's getting at?' Then he would probably note the quotation at the end which Jesus uses to describe the harvest time. It comes from an old poem (Joel 3.11–13) about the 'Holy War' against foreigners that the freedom-fighters talked about, but it turns the old poem upside-down and makes its words carry a very different meaning indeed. Then they would notice that the poem is about the secret, gentle way in which the wheat grows and goes on growing right up to the time of harvest. There is nothing violent in this process, until the very moment when the farmer puts in his sickle and the harvest is reaped.

But when would that moment come? Many of Jesus' stories about 'God's Way', beginning 'The kingdom of God is like . . .' pointed to the arrival of that kingdom, to the moment when the climax was reached. The farmer in the story above waits for exactly the right moment before harvesting. The trader who wants to buy the best pearl has to do so before he loses it to someone else. An urgent decision is needed. Has the right moment arrived? Jesus' mission was to urge the Jews to recognise that God's rule was in fact beginning and was beginning with Jesus' own work in their midst.

'It is by means of God's power that I drive out demons, and this proves that the kingdom of God has already come to you.'
(Luke 11.20)

The stories then were designed to help or even force people to make a choice about God's kingdom, but they were stories too which tried to help people see what God was like. God is king, said Jesus and that was a description of God with which all his countrymen would agree, but he was a king with a difference, as Jesus illustrated with another of his stories.

'There was a man who was giving a great feast, to which he invited many people. When it was time for the feast he sent his servant to tell his guests, "Come, everything is ready!" But they all began, one after another, to make excuses. The first one told the servant, "I have bought a field and must go and look at it; please accept my apologies." Another one said, "I have bought five pairs of oxen and am on my way to try them out; please accept my apologies." Another one said, "I have just got married and for that reason I cannot come."

The servant went back and told all this to his master. The master was furious and said to his servant. "Hurry out to the streets and alleys of the town and bring back the poor, the crippled, the blind, and the lame." Soon the servant said, "Your order has been carried out, sir, but there is room for more." So the master said to the servant, "Go out to the country roads and lanes and make people come in, so that my house will be full. I tell you all that none of those men who were invited will taste my dinner." '   (Luke 14.16–24)

When you realise that for the Jewish people a picture of God's kingdom was of a feast in which they all shared, you can see how sharp-edged Jesus' story was. God was king, yes, but his own people, whom he had invited, refused to come. In that case, the poorest and the weakest from everywhere should be invited in their stead, not only Jews but the 'heathen' as well. For Jesus had seen that God was the king of all, not of the Jews alone. It was a story that was bound to create enemies, but Jesus was fully aware of this.

'I came to set the earth on fire, and how I wish it were already kindled! I have a baptism to receive, and how distressed I am until it is over! Do you suppose that I came to bring peace to the world? Not peace, but division.'   (Luke 12.49–51)

God was also a Judge-King, said Jesus, and again he told stories which showed the kind of Judge-King God might be.

'... the people of all the nations will be gathered before him. Then he will divide them into two groups, just as a shepherd separates the sheep from the goats. He will put the righteous people on his right and the others on his left. Then the king will say to the people on his right, "Come, you who are blessed by my Father! Come and possess the kingdom which has been prepared for you ever since the creation of the world. I was hungry and you fed me, thirsty and you gave me drink; I was a stranger and you received me in your homes, naked and you clothed me ... whenever you did this for the least important of these brothers of mine, you did it for me." '   (Matthew 25.32–36, 40)

Again, there is no special place for the 'chosen people' in this judgement, no special privilege. God's judgement is conditioned by the way people had treated the poorest and those in real need. But Jesus had a warning about judgement too, which he put into a very memorable saying.

'Do not judge others, and God will not judge you; do not condemn others, and God will not condemn you; forgive others, and God will forgive you. Give to others, and God will give to you. Indeed, you will receive a full measure, a generous helping, poured into your hands – all that you can hold. The measure you use for others is the one that God will use for you.'

(Luke 6.37–38)

To say this to a society ruled by burdensome laws and, therefore, by fine and intricate judgements was again a courageous and bold thing to do. In case he had not made the point, Jesus used exaggeration to clinch the argument.

'Why do you look at the speck in your brother's eye, but pay no attention to the log in your own eye? How can you say to your brother, "Please, brother, let me take that speck out of your eye" yet can not even see the log in your own eye? You hypocrite! First take the log out of your own eye, and then you will be able to see clearly to take the speck out of your brother's eye.'   (Luke 6.41–42)

This was as good as saying to his Jewish countrymen that they were 'blind'. But even if they were 'blind' there was a chance, if they wanted it, to be given back their sight. No wonder that he also laid such emphasis upon 'repentance', upon change. The arrogant and the proud would have to become humble. Even his disciples did not understand what Jesus was saying about this.

An argument broke out among the disciples as to which one of them was the greatest. Jesus knew what they were thinking, so he took a child, stood him by his side, and said to them,

'Whoever welcomes this child in my name welcomes me; and whoever welcomes me, also welcomes the one who sent me. For he who is least among you all is the greatest.'

(Luke 9.46–48)

This theme of humility, of serving others, is one that echoes and re-echoes around Jesus' teaching.

It can all be summed up in a story about Jesus which we find in the Fourth Gospel. The whole of this gospel is concerned with making clear what Jesus stood for, and when the main part of his story has been told and John comes to tell us about the last days of Jesus, he begins with an episode which is immensely important. It is as if John is saying to his readers, 'All I have been saying about Jesus is made clear in this story; this reveals the nature of the man whose trial and execution I am about to recount.' Here is the story John chose:

Jesus and his disciples were at supper . . . (Jesus) rose from the table, took off his outer garment, and tied a towel round his waist. Then he poured some water into a basin and began to wash the disciples' feet and dry them with the towel round his waist . . . After Jesus had washed their feet, he put his outer garment back on and returned to his place at the table. 'Do you understand what I have just done to you?' he asked. 'You call me Teacher and Lord, and it is right that you do so, because that is what I am. I, your Lord and Teacher, have just washed your feet. You, then, should wash one another's feet. I have set an example for you, so that you will do just what I have done for you.'

(John 13.2, 4–5, 12–15)

This then, for Jesus, was God's way. It was a way of serving others, of caring for them, of being mindful of their good. He did not pretend that this way of living would be easy, indeed he said that it would take all a man's courage and determination and steadfastness, but in the end it was the only way of living that mattered, because it was God's way.

In Jesus' teaching, then, God was King, Judge and Servant, but above all else he was 'Father' (Abba). This was not a new idea to Judaism. It had been present in the prophets, the psalmists and the wise men for centuries, but Jesus gave it an intimacy which was quite new. He prayed to God as his Father and told his followers to do the same:

'When you pray, go to your room, close the door and pray to your Father, who is unseen. And your Father, who sees what you do in private, will reward you.'   (Matthew 6.6)

And when he was going through the agony of waiting for his trial and death in the garden of Gethsemane he cried out to God in these words:

'My Father, if it is possible, take this cup of suffering from me! Yet not what I want, but what you want.'   (Matthew 26.39)

How Jesus had come to know God in such close and familiar ways must wait for another chapter, but we can say with certainty that, for Jesus, God was indeed his 'Father' and it was this profound and urgent awareness of God which underlay all that he said and did.

6

Jesus the healer and miracle-worker

In the typical day in the life of Jesus which we looked at in Chapter 3, it is quite clear that Jesus' teaching and his healing go hand in hand. You cannot divide the healing from the teaching and merely say 'Jesus was a great teacher', nor divide the teaching from the healing and say 'Jesus was just a healer'. The two are inseparable. Because we are used to the ideas of twentieth-century medicine, it is difficult for us to get back into the thought-patterns and beliefs of people at the time of Jesus and see how they thought of healing. We are naturally sceptical of anything that smacks of the 'miraculous' and we want to know 'how' things work. It must be said at the outset that there is no means open to us of deciding on historical grounds whether or not what Jesus did was 'miraculous'. We simply do not have sufficient evidence. All we can do is to see Jesus' healing work in the context of his time and then see what his contemporaries thought of him.

It must be noted first of all that doctors were not very highly regarded during Old Testament times. In fact there are very, very few references to them. Healing was thought to be something that God alone gave and was, therefore, more to do with the priests and prophets than with anyone else. There were various rules laid down for what you should do if you were ill. If you thought you had leprosy, for example, you had to go to a priest for a diagnosis, and to a priest when you thought you might have been cured. He certified that you were 'clean' rather than 'unclean'.

Basically, diseases – or indeed injuries – were seen as being due to sin. That is, the person had offended God by not living in the right kind of way and his illness was a punishment. It was believed that underlying all this sin, the root cause of it, if you like, was the devil. He in turn had various 'helpers' – demons or evil spirits – who 'possessed' the sick person, and the person could only be made 'whole' if the evil spirits were driven out and the man received cleansing and forgiveness.

As you can see, for us this way of regarding illness seems very strange, but to Jesus and his contemporaries the relationship between sin and illness was a very close one. The very first healing mentioned in Mark's gospel illustrates this – it is a demon-possessed man who confronts Jesus and even seems to recognise who he is: 'I know who you are; you are God's holy messenger.' Jesus then commands the demon, 'Be quiet and come out of the man.'

One of the fascinating things to note here is that Jesus does not follow the customs of other exorcists of his day. (An exorcist is a person who claims to be able to drive out demons.) They used a whole series of rituals and incantations, including naming the authority by which they performed the exorcism. Jesus, in this story, does nothing like that. He simply orders the demon to leave. There are no incantations, no appeals to authority. It is a simple, straightforward command.

The other thing which is interesting is that Jesus seems to use two methods of healing. Sometimes he uses words alone, but in other cases of sickness he lays his hands on people.

A man suffering from a dreaded skin-disease came to Jesus, knelt down, and begged him for help. 'If you want to,' he said, 'you can make me clean.'

Jesus was filled with pity, and stretched out his hand and touched him. 'I do want to,' he answered. 'Be clean!'   (Mark 1.40–41)

And then Jesus, following the established custom of the day, tells the man to go to the priest.

'Let him examine you; then in order to prove to everyone that you are cured offer the sacrifice that Moses ordered.'   (Mark 1.44)

The relationship between illness and forgiveness was something to which Jesus some-times drew attention and sometimes ignored completely. In the case of the paralysed man let down through the roof by his friends, Jesus is completely explicit.

Seeing how much faith they had, Jesus said to the paralysed man, 'My son, your sins are forgiven'

And only when that had been said and there had been some dispute about Jesus' authority to forgive sins did he give the command that made the man whole 'Get up, pick up your mat, and go home!' (Mark 2.5, 11)

On another occasion, though, when he is asked about the relationship between sin and illness he contradicts the normal thinking of his time:

As Jesus walked along he saw a man who had been born blind. His disciples asked him 'Teacher, whose sin caused him to be born blind? Was it his own or his parents' sin?' Jesus answered, 'His blindness has nothing to do with his sin or his parents' sins.'

(John 9.1–3)

There were times, too, when Jesus used methods of healing which were similar to those of his contemporaries. Saliva was considered to have medicinal properties and so when Jesus healed the blind man at Bethsaida he spat on the man's eyes, then placed his hands on him and asked him 'Can you see anything?' The man looked up and said, 'I can see people but they look like trees walking about.' So Jesus placed his hands on the man again and this time he saw everything clearly. (Mark 8. 24–25)

When you read the stories about Jesus' healings in the gospels, it is always worth noting where they actually occur, that is, what the episodes are which precede and follow them. Often the gospel writers interweave healing stories with other stories so that they shed light on each other. The granting of sight to the blind man at Bethsaida is a case in point. This is pre-ceded by a story about the disciples not understanding, not 'seeing' who Jesus was, and it is followed by Peter's declaration that Jesus was the Messiah, i.e. the moment when the disciples 'saw' who Jesus really was.

There can be no doubt that his contemporaries acknowledged Jesus as a healer, even though the Pharisees tried to suggest that his healing power came not from God but from Beelzebub – the prince of devils. Jesus dealt with that suggestion very firmly:

'How can Satan drive out Satan? . . . If Satan's kingdom divides into groups, it cannot last, but will fall apart and come to an end.'   (Mark 3.22, 26)

Jesus seemed to be aware, however, that his healing power could easily be misunderstood. One of the problems he faced throughout his ministry was that people might see him only as a magician or wonder-worker.

Some Pharisees came to Jesus and started to argue with him. They wanted to trap him, so they asked him to perform a miracle to show that God approved of him.

But Jesus gave a deep groan and said, 'Why do the people of this day ask for a miracle? No, I tell you! No such proof will be given to these people!'   (Mark 8.11–12)

He did not want people to regard him in this way at all – he wanted them to see his healings as 'signs', hints, suggestions, indications that God's reign was beginning.

Jesus, then, was seen by his contemporaries as a healer filled with God's power, following the tradition of exorcism and healings in the Jewish faith, but doing so in such a way that his healings were 'signals' of God's presence.

If today we find it difficult to understand the healing miracles, we may well find it doubly difficult to understand what are sometimes called the 'Nature Miracles'. It will be worth looking at two of these in some detail in order to try to see what is going on.

The first story (you can find it in Mark 6. 34–44) is the 'Feeding of the Five Thousand'.

When Jesus got out of the boat, he saw this large crowd, and his heart was filled with pity for them, because they were like sheep without a shepherd. So he began to teach them many things. When it was getting late, his disciples came to him and said, 'It is already very late, and this is a lonely place. Send the people away, and let them go to the nearby farms and villages in order to buy themselves something to eat.'

'You yourselves give them something to eat,' Jesus answered.

They asked, 'Do you want us to go and spend 200 silver coins on bread in order to feed them?'

So Jesus asked them, 'How much bread have you got? Go and see.'

When they found out, they told him, 'Five loaves and also two fish.'

Jesus then told his disciples to make all the people divide into groups and sit down on the green grass. So the people sat down in rows, in groups of a hundred and groups of fifty. Then Jesus took the five loaves and the two fish, looked up to heaven, and gave thanks to God. He broke the loaves and gave them to his disciples to distribute to the people. He also divided the two fish among them all. Everyone ate and had enough. Then the disciples took up 12 baskets full of what was left of the bread and of the fish. The number of men who were fed was five thousand.

It's a strange but well-known story and the interpretations of it are many. Some claim that it was a kind of gathering of freedom-fighters: after all, they sat in ranks like an army, and in the version of the story in John's gospel it says 'they wanted to make Jesus their king.' Others say that it was an ordinary gathering in which, after Jesus had taught the people, they felt bound to share their food with each other. Yet others say the story has been very heavily influenced by two stories from the Old Testament – the first concerning Moses who gave his people bread in the wilderness and led them out of slavery into a new life; and the second concerning Elisha who distributed 20 barley loaves and a little fresh grain among 100 men so that 'they all ate and had some left' (2 Kings 4.42–44); in this interpretation perhaps the feeding was designed to show that Jesus fulfilled both the Law (Moses) and the prophets (Elisha). There are interpretations of the feeding story which say that it was a kind of eucharistic meal in which tiny pieces of bread were shared – and, in fact, if you look at the account of the Last Supper you will see that there too Jesus took bread, gave thanks, broke the bread and shared it.

All of these interpretations are possible. One thing is certain – that at this stage in time we simply cannot tell what happened on that hillside 2,000 years ago. The story has become too much 'shaped' by tradition and interpretation for us to begin to get back to any definite historical core. Whatever you may think of it now it was clearly a very important story for the early Christians because versions of it are found in each of the four gospels.

It is followed in Mark's gospel by another nature miracle, that is, Jesus walking on the water. Again we cannot know what, if anything, happened. We are naturally and properly hesitant over accounts such as this, seeing them as possible exaggeration. We have to say too that when we try to decide whether this kind of story is historically genuine, we have to take into account what Jesus said about not being prepared to perform miracles as a means of proof.

We would probably do well to approach this story of walking on the water as a 'description' or 'interpretation' of Jesus. The Jewish people had always seen the sea as a symbol of chaos and evil. It was for them a raging, troublesome and terrifying thing – to be avoided as far as possible.

The story seems to suggest that Jesus conquered the power of chaos and that he trod evil under his feet. The fact that Mark follows this story with a general account of Jesus healing the sick and casting out demons suggests that the story was being used here for allegorical purposes, whatever its historical basis may have been.

However we think of the 'nature miracles' or the 'healings', one of the central things that comes across from all of them is that Jesus was a man of considerable authority. He was a man of great power and strength. A man of total and absolute integrity. He had a mission to fulfil, to proclaim by deed and word that God's rule was beginning, that God was at work amongst his people. Even if you find the healings and the nature miracles difficult to believe, you need to ask yourself another question, 'What kind of man must Jesus have been to have had such stories told about him?'

7

Stories of Jesus' birth

The question of where Jesus had come from was one that did not seem to trouble his earliest followers unduly. Mark's gospel, for example, has no mention at all of Jesus' birth; it begins starkly when Jesus is approximately 30 years of age. For Mark, all that had happened up to that time was unimportant. John's gospel is equally lacking. He begins by exploring the meaning of Jesus as the 'Word' of God. He has nothing about angels or kings or shepherds. If you want to find all the normal ingredients of the Christmas story you will have to look at Matthew's gospel and at Luke's. Matthew's introduction of Jesus' birth is fairly simply handled, or so it seems.

> 'This was how the birth of Jesus Christ took place. His mother Mary was engaged to Joseph, but before they were married, she found out that she was going to have a baby by the Holy Spirit.' ·
> (Matthew 1.18)

In Luke's gospel the story is much more complicated. It is connected with the birth of John the Baptist. There are visits by angels. The birth, it is said, will be the result of Mary conceiving a child by the Holy Spirit and that birth and the birth of John the Baptist (Jesus' cousin, according to Luke) will be inextricably linked. Mary sings a song of triumph, as does John the Baptist's father, Zechariah.

What are we to make of all this? Did things actually happen in the way Matthew and Luke said, or are their stories simply a way of trying to say 'Jesus was a great and wonderful man sent by God to be the Saviour of God's people?' Let us have a look at each of the versions: Matthew's first.

Matthew begins his gospel in this way: 'This is the list of the ancestors of Jesus Christ, who was a descendant of David, who was a descendant of Abraham' and then follows a long table about who was the father of whom. It's a kind of genealogy, or family tree. Now the word translated here as 'list of ancestors' literally means 'beginning', and could be taken in any one of four ways. It may indeed refer to the genealogy which follows, or it may refer to the actual birth of Jesus. It could on the other hand mean 'life-story', or it could even mean 'the new creation' which begins at the birth of Jesus.

It would be tedious to go through every word of Matthew's introduction in this way, but it does go to show that what at first sight seems a simple 'historical' record may have many other strands of meaning woven through it. Another example of this can be seen in the way Matthew describes Jesus. He calls him 'Christ' (which is the Greek word for 'Messiah'/ 'anointed one'), 'Son of David' and 'Son of Abraham'. Now, if you look carefully at the genealogical table, you will see that Matthew divides it into three equal parts: from Abraham to David, from David to the deportation (in 587 BC large numbers of Jews were deported to Babylon as members of a conquered nation) and from the deportation to the birth of Jesus Christ.

You may see, then, that Matthew has imposed a kind of pattern upon his material. He is trying to convey something to his readers, perhaps about the orderly nature of God's activities, suggesting that it is as part of this order and progress that God's chosen one appears. If you look here for what we call 'history', you might well be looking for the wrong kind of information.

Then Matthew tells the story of the coming of the Magi: the astrologers from the East. This story does not appear in any other place, so we have no other evidence to check it against. We cannot therefore be sure how much historical accuracy there is in the episode. What we do know is that there are echoes of the Moses story contained within it (as there are in many later episodes in Matthew's gospel). Moses at the exodus led the people out of Egypt, even though the Pharaoh was unco-operative. Here it is Herod the king who is unco-operative, while Jesus is seen to be a new kind of Moses. Originally Moses was taken out of Egypt for safety; here Jesus goes to Egypt for safety and then returns.

Again, we cannot know how accurate any of this is, although interestingly enough there has been considerable speculation amongst astronomers about the star which features in the story. Some claim that it was a 'super-nova', for which they say there is evidence in Chinese astronomical records; others say that Jupiter and Saturn came close together, as it were, in an unusual conjunction.

Apart from these strange stories of kings and stars and travellings to and from Egypt, Matthew says nothing about Jesus' early life, except that he grew up in Nazareth. Between early childhood and adulthood in Matthew's version there is a total gap.

We are no better off when it comes to Luke's story. In Luke there is also a mingling of history and symbolism in which we find it difficult to sift out what is a 'true' record of what happened and what has been added in order to emphasise the 'truth'. Luke, however, as we have seen, makes the birth of John the Baptist an important event in his story. It was believed that when the Messiah came, one of the great prophets would return in order to announce that coming. It would seem that Luke saw John the Baptist in that kind of role.

John's father, Zechariah, was one of the priests entitled to officiate at the temple sacrifices, but because there were so many priests they had to draw lots as to who should 'burn incense'. Incense was thought of as a symbol of people's prayers rising to God, and after burning the incense Zechariah would be expected to return to say God's blessing to the people. It was during this time that Luke says Zechariah saw an 'angel'. The word 'angel' for us conjures up pictures of tall and rather elegant white beings with human features and enormous wings. In fact the word 'angel' simply means 'messenger', but because people thought that God was utterly holy and distant, they imagined that he must have 'messengers' who flew to and from the earth to tell people what to do. It was such a messenger that

Zechariah says talked to him, announcing that the child for whom he longed would be the new Elijah.

Luke then weaves the story of John's arrival into the threads of the story of Jesus' own birth, which equally is prophesied by an angelic messenger. Also, as in Zechariah's case, the angel tells Mary what her son shall be called – Jesus. For the Jewish people at that time 'naming' was a tremendously important activity, because the name was thought somehow to be bound up with the person's inner character. If you knew a person's name you 'knew' them completely.

The story then proceeds with an account of a Roman census which Luke says took place during the reign of the Emperor Augustus, when Quirinius was Governor of Syria. Here we come up against a difficulty. We know that Herod died in 4 BC and we know that P. Sulpicius Quirinius became proconsul of Syria in AD 6. We cannot 'marry' the two dates, so we have to assume that in the stories of Jesus' birth such 'historical' details are not to be seen as being terribly important. It may be that Luke mentioned the census (which was the basis of the Roman taxation system) as a way of emphasising that Jesus was the Messiah, the one who would liberate his people from the Roman yoke. Then, in Luke's account, shepherds come to worship the infant Jesus. This event may have been included as a symbol to show that shepherds (who were regarded by the orthodox as people who neglected their religious duties) were the representatives of all those hundreds of ordinary, humble, poor people who later recognised Jesus. In the same kind of way the fact that when Mary and Joseph arrived in Bethlehem there was 'no room for them in the inn' may have been intended to symbolise the rejection of Jesus by the majority of his fellow-countrymen.

In Matthew and in Luke, then, history, story, symbol, legend, prophecy and poetry are all intertwined. We have to read the stories not as straightforward recordings of what actually happened, but as attempts to demonstrate what an extraordinary and significant person Jesus was.

8

Stories about Jesus' adult life

As we have seen, we cannot discover much about the childhood years of Jesus' life. In all the gospels, except Luke's, there is silence until Jesus is a man. In Luke there is the story of Jesus going up to the Temple as a twelve year old with his parents and debating with the learned scholars of his day. At the age of 12 a Jewish boy becomes 'bar Mitzvah' that is, a 'Son of the Law', thereby becoming also aware of the Fatherhood of God. This is reflected in this story of Jesus' 'coming of age'.

The gospels may not be agreed about Jesus' birth or early childhood, but what they are all most certainly at pains to demonstrate is the central importance of John the Baptist in Jesus' early ministry. As we have said earlier, expectations about the coming of the Messiah were at fever-pitch and the arrival of John the Baptist like a prophet of old must have been seen by many as a signal of that Coming. John was an ascetic, that is, a holy man living a rigorous and austere life out in the wilderness, calling people to repent. Nothing is known of his early years apart from the story of his birth nor of the beliefs which led him to perform his extraordinary task. As has been said previously, some scholars think that he may have had some links with the Essene communities, but in the gospels he bursts into the story in a most sudden and dramatic fashion. Like Jesus he too acquired a group of disciples (they are mentioned in the gospels as coming to Jesus to talk with him), and he too seems to have taught his disciples a special prayer of their own.

In fact, according to Luke's account, John the Baptist not only taught his disciples a prayer; he gave the people a code of moral teaching too:
'Whoever has two shirts' he said, 'must give one to the man who has none, and whoever has food must share it.'

Some tax collectors came to be baptised, and they asked him: 'Teacher, what are we to do?'

'Don't collect more than is legal,' he told them.

Some soldiers also asked him, 'What about us? What are we to do?'

'Don't take money from anyone by force or accuse anyone falsely. Be content with your pay.' (Luke 3.11–14)

It must be remembered though that this message for social and moral reform was in the context of the coming judgement. John talked about sorting 'the wheat from the chaff'. It was an old picture and one with which his hearers would be only too familiar. His task was to prepare his people, to remind them as forcefully as possible that they needed to repent, to change, so that they would be ready for the Messiah when he came.

John the Baptist re-appears in the gospel stories when he speaks his mind to Herod Antipas about the latter's immoral ways. It was this that was his undoing. Herod imprisoned him in the fortress of Machaerus to the east of the Dead Sea and there beheaded him.

Sometime before that, when the news of this strange prophetic figure reached Nazareth, Jesus went off into the wilderness to find him. Mark speaks about this moment in Jesus' life like this:

> Jesus came from Nazareth, in the region of Galilee, and was baptised by John in the Jordan. As soon as Jesus came up out of the water, he saw heaven opening and the Spirit coming down on him like a dove. And a voice came from heaven, 'You are my own dear Son. I am pleased with you.'
> (Mark 1.9–11)

Whatever you make of the stories of Jesus' early childhood, there can be no doubt that his baptism in the river Jordan was profoundly important for him. It marked the turning point in his life, From being a carpenter-cum-builder in an obscure town, he became a teacher and exorcist, a healer and preacher. We can have no means of knowing what actually happened to Jesus' understanding of himself at his Baptism, but whatever it was he came to realise that he had an intense awareness of God as his Father and a longing to do his Father's will. Whilst it may have been a supreme religious experience for Jesus, the net immediate effect was to drive him away from all his family and friends. He went into the hills of the wilderness to be alone; to think things through, to pray and agonise about what he had to do. Mark puts it like this:

> At once the Spirit made him go into the desert, where he stayed forty days, being tempted by Satan. Wild animals were there also, and angels came and helped him.
> (Mark 1.12–13)

It is a stark, but strangely ominous description. Mark is saying that Jesus battled with the powers of evil in the wilderness, that there was a real trial of strength. It was the opening battle in the war between good (in the person of Jesus) and evil which was to rage throughout Jesus' ministry. 'The wild animals' is probably not a reference to evil powers, but to the belief that a good man was not harmed by wild creatures. It may be that Mark was suggesting that Jesus had begun to restore the conditions of paradise in which, when evil had been banished, man and beast would live together in perfect peace and harmony.

There was another episode in Jesus' life besides his baptism in which he seemed to have an intense and extraordinary experience. Here is Luke's description of it:

> About a week after he had said these things, Jesus took Peter, John and James with him and went up a hill to pray. While he was praying, his face changed its appearance and his clothes became dazzling white. Suddenly two men were there talking with him. They were Moses and Elijah, who appeared in heavenly glory and talked with Jesus about the way in which he would soon fulfil God's purpose by dying in Jerusalem. Peter and his companions were sound asleep, but they awoke and saw Jesus' glory and the two men who were standing with him. As the men were leaving Jesus, Peter said to him: 'Master, how good it is that we are here. We will make three tents, one for you, one for Moses and one for Elijah.' (He did not really know what he was saying.) While he was still speaking, a cloud appeared and covered them with its

shadow, and the disciples were afraid as the cloud came over them. A voice said from the cloud 'This is my Son, whom I have chosen – listen to him!'

When the voice stopped, there was Jesus all alone. The disciples kept quiet about all this, and told no one at that time anything they had seen. (Luke 9. 28–36)

Luke is saying that Jesus went up the mountain to pray (the mountain may have been Mount Hermon) and there Jesus was somehow transformed. There are those who say that this kind of physical transformation does sometimes come over very holy people when they are praying very, very deeply and they claim therefore that this story about Jesus may be an accurate portrayal of a real event. Others say that the episode was probably one which the disciples experienced after Jesus' resurrection, but was put in this place in the gospels as a foretaste of things to come; and yet others say it is a kind of Christian legend. It is probably fair to suggest that it is something nearer history than legend. It may be that Jesus foresaw some kind of spiritual battle (not unlike the one he was to face in the garden of Gethsemane when again Peter, James and John were with him) in which he would have to face the prospect of dying in the service of God his Father. Unlike Moses and Elijah who, tradition had it, had been translated bodily into heaven, Jesus was having to embrace the possibility of death as a way of being a faithful servant.

Matthew and Mark recount the same incident, and in all three versions of the story it is preceded by Jesus telling his disciples about his suffering.
'If anyone wants to come with me, he must first carry his cross, and follow me. For whoever wants to save his own life will lose it; but whoever loses his life for my sake will find it.'
(Matthew 16. 24–25)

It would seem likely, then, that at his Baptism Jesus became intensely aware of God as his Father and the message he had to proclaim. At the Transfiguration he came finally to accept that death was the only way in which he could live out that message in its entirety. Both Baptism and Transfiguration were experiences which moulded the way in which Jesus understood who God was and what God required him to do.

We have seen how the gospel writers tried to convey by story, legend, poetry and history who Jesus was and where he came from. Two of them, Matthew and Luke, do this by means of fascinating stories of his childhood; two, Mark and John, by concentrating upon his Baptism; and three, Mark, Matthew and Luke, by telling of his Transfiguration. They, however, were writing about Jesus long after his death. Jesus' immediate friends had to try to decide who he was whilst he was alive and talking with them. At one point Jesus asked quite specifically for his disciples' decision.
On the way he asked them 'Tell me, who do people say I am?'

'Some say that you are John the Baptist,' they answered, 'others say that you are Elijah, while others say that you are one of the prophets.'

'What about you?' he asked them. 'Who do you say I am?'

Peter answered, 'You are the Messiah'.

(Mark 8.27–29)

It was a straightforward though momentous decision on Peter's part, but in a way the choice Peter faced was that faced by everyone who met Jesus. He was not someone you could ignore. You had to decide one way or the other what you thought about him, what you thought about his teachings. A person of such strength often makes enemies and Jesus was no exception. He had challenged the accepted social and religious customs of his day. He had told people of their duty to love and forgive. He had healed the sick, cared for the poor and the outcast and had suggested by means of his example and his teachings that people, if they followed his way, could transform the world. The more he taught, though, the greater became the divide in people's opinions about him.

Inevitably the time came when that division hardened and the decision was made to get rid of Jesus once and for all. It is to the description of the last weeks in Jesus' life that we now turn.

9

Facing the capital city

Rumours about Jesus must have reached Jerusalem, the capital city, almost as soon as he began his ministry. It is highly likely that he himself visited Jerusalem a number of times. One of his poems is about the city and in it Jesus seems to be saying that he had been there more than once.

'Jerusalem, Jerusalem! You kill the prophets and stone the messengers God has sent you! How many times have I wanted to put my arms round all your people, just as a hen gathers her chicks under her wings, but you would not let me!' (Matthew 23.37)

But his main work had been in the north of the country, in the Galilee, and there his work had begun to draw to a close, for when the religious leaders and the freedom-fighters had really begun to grasp what he stood for, neither group would have any more to do with him. The issue between Jesus and his countrymen had become very clear. It was a question about the leadership of the Jewish people and what God wanted them to become. Jesus believed that God had sent him not just to talk to his countrymen, but to lead them. But he was not the kind of leader that the Pharisees or the freedom-fighters or the common people wanted. So Jesus decided that, whatever happened in Galilee, he must make one last appeal to his people and face them and the government in Jerusalem itself. He may also have decided that the great Passover festival held in the spring would be the best time to appeal to them.

At that festival the city would be crowded. There would be crowds there from all over Palestine; but more than that, there would also be crowds from the Jewish communities all over the world. This was the festival that all Jews tried to attend at some time in their lives. It was the festival when they remembered how, long ago, God had called them out of Egypt, led them across the desert and given them their homeland. The festival was celebrated in Jewish homes all over the world; but it was a wonderful thing to be able to celebrate it in Jerusalem itself. So it was in Jerusalem, Jesus decided, he would appeal to his people to be the kind of people God wanted them to be.

His journey south from Galilee to Jerusalem possibly took as long as six months. At the beginning of his account of these last days of Jesus' life Mark tells us that he not only spent some time in Judaea but also 'crossed the Jordan river'. He goes on: 'Again crowds came flocking to him and he taught them as he always did.' (Mark 10.1)

Whenever it was that Jesus actually came to Jerusalem, he was taking a very dangerous step. Jerusalem was very different from the Galilee. In the city were the headquarters of the Jewish government, led by the Sadducees; and here, during the various festivals, the Roman governor came with his legionaries to see that there was no rioting or rebellion. Jesus knew that the Sadducees would be no friends of his – they did not want to see any change and they intended to keep on the right side of the Roman government. They were not likely to let him talk to the crowds in the Temple as he had talked to the villagers in Galilee. At the very hint of any kind of 'rebellion' the Roman governor would step in without asking any questions, and if the Romans stepped in there was only one punishment for rebels and slaves – a terrible and cruel execution: being nailed on a cross and left to die a lingering death, at the mercy of carrion birds.

But Jesus knew that crowds are uncertain – you can never be sure which way they will go. The Jewish authorities in Jerusalem knew that they were not loved by the common people nor by many of the Pharisees. The crowds might soon turn against them. They would have to go carefully in handling Jesus. He might therefore have a chance to proclaim his message after all.

Jesus, as we have seen, had used stories for a lot of his teachings. He had also once or twice used what we can only call 'acted stories'. This is something quite strange to us, but it is easy to see why he did it.

In the old days, the prophets had sometimes used 'acted stories'. They took some incident – the sort of thing that would perhaps often happen without anybody taking much notice of it – and acted it out in such a way that people were forced to take notice of it. And when people began to notice what the prophet was doing, they would soon see that his actions were intended to mean much more than they would ordinarily mean.

For example, take what Jeremiah once did. There was a rubbish dump outside the city of Jerusalem. It was reached through the Potsherd Gate – a gate so called because it was near the potters' shops and they threw their broken pots on the dump. Rubbish was also burned there. There were often crowds standing near the gate. So Jeremiah took an earthenware flask, broke it and said to the people: 'Thus says the Lord of Hosts: So will I break this people and this city, as one breaks a potter's vessel, so that it can never be mended.'

Jeremiah was saying to the people of Jerusalem that since they had refused to live in God's way, God was not going to have them as his people any longer. Words alone had not impressed them, but Jeremiah thought an 'acted story' like this would have some real impact.

Perhaps what Jeremiah had done was in Jesus' mind as he came to the city. We know that he had read Jeremiah very carefully – he once used Jeremiah's words in a poem of his own.

The first of Jesus' acted stories was his ride into the city, often called Jesus' 'triumphal entry'. It has this name because from the very earliest days Christian preachers have used this story as a picture of Jesus as a sort of king. But if it had been a public claim to kingship and a royal ride into the city, the police would have moved in very quickly. That was just the sort of evidence they were looking for. It could easily have been made to look like an act of rebellion

– and Pilate, the Roman governor, would have wasted no time in dealing with him.

Jesus' 'ride' was part of an act of worship. If it was in the October that he first came to Jerusalem (which does at least seem possible) then the festival would have been the Festival of the Tents, when the Jewish people celebrated their march through the desert after they had been rescued from Egypt. It was also their Harvest Festival. At that festival, palm branches were carried from Jericho and the procession rounded the Mount of Olives on its way to the Temple. As the city came into sight, the pilgrims chanted words from Psalm 118:
'May God bless the one who comes in the name of the Lord!
From the Temple of the Lord we bless you.'

Jesus and his friends joined the pilgrims. But Jesus had arranged with a friend for a donkey to be ready for him if he wanted it. No doubt his friends (as we shall see) still thought of Jesus as the deliverer of his country and its rightful ruler. But Jesus deliberately rode on a farm animal as a sign of peace to show what his leadership meant. Perhaps he remembered how his ancestor King David rode back along this same road to claim his throne again after a rebellion against him (see 2 Samuel 19.41–20.3). King David rode on a war-horse; Jesus rode on a donkey. It is not likely that the crowd took much notice of these Galilean pilgrims and what they were doing. Later on, in Christian preaching, the event became a favourite story of an impressive public ride into the city. But at the time itself Jesus' main concern was to make his peaceful intentions as clear as he could to his own friends.

The second 'acted story' was in the full gaze of the crowds and the Jewish authorities. The Foreigners' Court in the Temple was the area where foreigners were permitted to go and was intended for their use, if they wished (as some foreigners did) to share in the Temple worship. But it was being used as a market and a short cut across the Temple to the city. Jesus again wanted to make clear that God's care was for everybody; the authorities were turning the Temple into their kind of Temple, not God's. So Jesus drove out the traders and over-turned their tables.

The Temple authorities could not ignore this act of open criticism of themselves. They met Jesus face to face in the temple courts.
...as he taught, the chief priests and the elders came to him and asked, 'What right have you to do these things? Who gave you this right?' Jesus answered them, 'I will ask you just one question and if you give me an answer, I will tell you what right I have to do these things. Where did John's right to baptise come from: was it from God or from man?'

They started to argue amongst themselves, 'What shall we say? If we answer "From God" he will say to us, "Why, then, did you not believe John?" But if we say "From man," we are afraid of what the people might do, because they are all convinced that John was a prophet!' So they answered Jesus, 'We don't know'.

And he said to them, 'Neither will I tell you, then, by what right I do these things.'
(Matthew 21.23–27)

Despite this rebuff, they had to find some kind of evidence that would enable them to arrest him and charge him with some crime. They must have known in their hearts that Jesus was not the sort of person to be guilty of any crime; but they also knew that he meant business and that he was challenging their right to be the leaders of the Jewish people. They must arrest him somehow.
'Teacher' (said the Pharisees and some of Herod's followers) 'we know that you tell the truth.

You teach the truth about God's will for man, without worrying about what people think, because you pay no attention to a man's status. Tell us, then, what do you think? Is it against our Law to pay taxes to the Roman Emperor or not?'

Jesus, however, was aware of their evil plan, and so he said, 'You hypocrites. Why are you trying to trap me? Show me the coin for paying the tax!'

They brought him the coin, and he asked them, 'Whose name and face are these?'

'The Emperor's,' they answered.

So Jesus said to them, 'Well, then, pay the Emperor what belongs to the Emperor, and pay God what belongs to God.'
(Matthew 22. 16–22)

It was clear, then, that Jesus was not going to be caught out easily, and the authorities had to move carefully. They were not sure how the crowd might take the open arrest of Jesus – or how the Galileans, known for their hot-headedness, would take what would seem to them to be an attack on another Galilean. But their minds were made up. Jesus must be stopped.

Even if it was October when all this happened, it seems that Jesus did not intend to make his final appeal to his nation at any festival other than the Passover Festival in the spring. He, therefore, slipped out of the Jerusalem government's control into the region across the River Jordan, which was King Herod's territory. Perhaps this is where he spent the winter and perhaps this is what Mark was referring to when he mentioned Jesus' work east of the Jordan.

One other incident very like an 'acted story' was remembered by the friends of Jesus concerning Jerusalem and the Temple.

As Jesus sat near the Temple treasury he watched the people as they dropped in their money. Many rich men dropped in a lot of money; then a poor widow came along and dropped in two little copper coins, worth about a penny. He called his disciples together and said to them, 'I tell you that this poor widow put more in the offering box than all the others. For the others put in what they had to spare of their riches; but she, poor as she is, put in all she had – she gave all she had to live on.'
(Mark 12.41)

Jesus had literally turned things upside-down in his acted story and you can see from the teaching about the widow that he turned people's ideas 'upside-down' as well. In the heart of the capital city he was claiming to show by his acted stories and his teaching what God was like and how God wanted man to live. It was indeed a challenge that had to be met sooner or later.

10

Real leadership, real kingship

Jesus must have realised very early on that his fellow-countrymen would not listen to him. He knew what the synagogues were like. He knew that there were many good people who worshipped there, but he also knew how narrow and rigid even good people's ideas can be.

The woman in the following story was probably a very good woman, full of good intentions. But notice Jesus' comment:

A woman spoke up from the crowd and said to him 'How happy is the woman who bore you and nursed you!'

But Jesus answered, 'Rather, how happy are those who hear the word of God and obey it!'   (Luke 11.27–28)

Jesus knew, too, that the religious leaders were more likely to resent what he said than really listen – or check what he did against what prophets like Amos and Jeremiah or even the Torah said. This story makes this plain.

One Sabbath Jesus went to eat a meal at the home of one of the leading Pharisees, and people were watching Jesus closely. A man whose legs and arms were swollen came to Jesus, and Jesus asked the teachers of the Law and the Pharisees, 'Does our Law allow healing on the Sabbath or not?'

But they would not say anything. Jesus took the man, healed him and sent him away. Then he said to them, 'If any one of you had a son or an ox that happened to fall in a well on a Sabbath, would you not pull him out at once on the Sabbath itself?'   (Luke 14.1–5)

To grow up with freedom-fighters as Jesus did in Galilee, sincere men though many of them were, was to realise how closed their minds were to anything but their own convictions; anybody who disagreed with them was a traitor.

Perhaps he hoped to the very end that his countrymen would listen. In those last days in Jerusalem – and Jesus knew they were his last days – he still appealed to them. Maybe, after all, the city he dearly loved would listen. For he did love Jerusalem, the city where he had first sensed his vocation as a boy. We know this from an incident which Luke includes in his account of Jesus' last days. He tells us that when Jesus was reaching the city, as he came round the Olive Hill and saw the city across the valley, 'his eyes filled with tears'.

But even if his fellow countrymen, the religious leaders and the freedom fighters were deaf to what he had to say, he hoped that at least his group of followers would understand.

When Jesus had begun his work in the Galilee, there had been some people who listened and became his friends. Perhaps they were the people who came back to ask questions after hearing him tell some of his stories.

Jesus had taken a very bold step with them. He had called some of them to leave their business and homes and form a small company of close friends. Here is Mark's account of what had happened:

As Jesus walked along the shore of Lake Galilee, he saw two fishermen, Simon and his brother Andrew, catching fish with a net. Jesus said to them, 'Come with me and I will teach you to catch men.' At once they left their nets and went with him.

He went a little farther on and saw two other brothers, James and John, the sons of Zebedee. They were in their boat getting their nets ready. As soon as Jesus saw them, he called them; so they left their father Zebedee in the boat with the hired men and went with Jesus.

(Mark 1.16–20)

These four friends became the inner core of a larger group: the Twelve.

Then Jesus went up a hill and called to himself the men he wanted. They came to him and he chose twelve who he named Apostles. 'I have chosen you to be with me,' he told them. 'I will also send you out to preach, and you will have authority to drive out demons.'

These are the twelve he chose: Simon (Jesus gave him the name Peter); James and his brother John, the sons of Zebedee (Jesus gave them the name Boanerges which means 'Men of Thunder'); Andrew, Philip, Bartholomew, Matthew, Thomas, James son of Alphaeus, Thaddaeus, Simon the Patriot and Judas Iscariot, who betrayed Jesus.   (Mark 3.13–19)

Jesus' group of close friends were all Galileans, except Judas who was a southerner from a village called Kerioth. They were mostly fishermen; one was a tax-collector. One was apparently a member of the freedom-fighters – Simon the 'Patriot' (another term for 'Zealot' is used here). They were a mixed group. Jesus called them, Mark says, 'to be with him' and to take part with him in the work in the villages.

But the important thing to notice is the name by which Jesus referred to them – 'The Twelve'. This does not mean that there were always exactly twelve men in this inner group of close friends. Indeed if we try to work out all their names we shall find that it is not easy to make their number come exactly to twelve. Numbers are often used as 'symbols' or tokens. The number 'Twelve' would recall to any Jewish person the number of the 'Twelve Tribes' that formed the beginning of the Hebrew nation when they entered their homeland. Palestine, in the twelfth century BC. When Jesus called his close friends 'The Twelve' he was calling these men together to begin a new venture in living as God's people. They were drawn from the common people of the Jewish nation to carry on what their nation itself – especially the religious leaders and freedom fighters – was refusing to do. They were bound together in a fellowship which had nothing now to do with national or racial matters, but simply by their loyalty to God – a loyalty anybody could show, whoever they were, by simply 'changing their minds' and 'trusting in the "Good News".' They shared with Jesus his work in Galilee and Jesus hoped they would share with him in whatever happened – even perhaps, face death itself with him.

42

On this small group of men, slow as they were to grasp what Jesus really stood for, Jesus rested the whole of his work. They were to be his 'apprentices' and learn how to live in God's way and how to help others to live in his way too.

What he wanted his 'apprentices' to do and how he wanted them to live is shown in this story of a man – a rich man – who wanted to become a friend of Jesus, but could not face up to the demands which Jesus made on him:

As Jesus was starting on his way again, a man ran up, knelt before him, and asked him, 'Good Teacher, what must I do to receive eternal life?'

'Why do you call me good?' Jesus asked him. 'No one is good except God alone. You know the commandments: "Do not commit murder; do not commit adultery; do not steal; do not accuse anyone falsely; do not cheat; respect your father and your mother." ' 'Teacher,' the man said, 'ever since I was young, I have obeyed all these commandments.'

Jesus looked straight at him with love and said, 'You need only one thing. Go and sell all you have and give the money to the poor and you will have riches in heaven; then come and follow me.' When the man heard this, gloom spread over his face, and he went away sad because he was very rich. (Mark 10.17–22)

How slow even his close friends were to 'change their minds' and see things through Jesus' eyes is shown by a story of their conversation at the last supper they had with Jesus – the supper on the night on which Jesus was arrested. This is Luke's account of what happened. Jesus had to repeat yet again what he must have said many, many times before: how hard it was for them to 'change their ways' and 'trust in the Good News'!

An argument broke out among the disciples as to which one of them should be thought of as the greatest. Jesus said to them, 'The kings of the pagans have power over their people ... But this is not the way it is with you; rather, the greatest one among you must be like the youngest, and the leader must be like the servant. Who is greater, the one who sits down to eat or the one who serves him? The one who sits down, of course. But I am among you as one who serves.' (Luke 22.24–27)*

This brings us to the final and most important 'acted story' that Jesus performed in those last days. This, like his riding into the city on a donkey, was performed to help his friends to grasp the meaning of all he was doing. Jesus knew that his death was not far off. His friends still stubbornly believed that Jesus would, by God's power, establish the Jewish empire which so many people longed for. How he would do this they did not know. Perhaps they thought God would miraculously intervene and come to their help; some of them, we know, were carrying arms. But Jesus was too clear-eyed to waste time wondering about what might happen. He knew God would vindicate him, but how God would vindicate him he left in God's hands. That it was death that he had to face he had no doubt. But his friends, with their conventional ideas about God's Chosen Leader still filling their minds, could not imagine that God would ever let him die.

At the supper table Jesus did something he had not done before. This is so important that we will hear two accounts of what happened; first of all, the earliest account by Paul (he mentions it in one of his letters); and then the account Mark gives us (his gospel was the earliest gospel to be written; he wrote it about AD 65-70).

---

*Notice also the similar teaching conveyed in the story of the washing of the disciples' feet, an event which took place at the same supper party.

Here is Paul's account:

For I received from the Lord the teaching that I passed on to you: that the Lord Jesus, on the night he was betrayed, took a piece of bread, gave thanks to God, broke it, and said, 'This is my body, which is for you. Do this in memory of me.' In the same way, after the supper he took the cup and said, 'This cup is God's new covenant, sealed with my blood. Whenever you drink it, do so in memory of me.'

This means that every time you eat this bread and drink from this cup you proclaim the Lord's death until he comes. (I Corinthians 11.23–26)

Here is Mark's account:

While they were eating, Jesus took a piece of bread, gave a prayer of thanks, broke it and gave it to his disciples. 'Take it', he said, 'this is my body.'

Then he took a cup, gave thanks to God, and handed it to them; and they all drank from it. Jesus said, 'This is my blood which is poured out for many, my blood which seals God's covenant. I tell you, I will never again drink this wine until the day I drink the new wine in the Kingdom of God.' (Mark 14.22–25)

This supper was to become the central act of Christian worship. The friends of Jesus, when they met regularly (as they did, to begin with) in order to have supper together, remembered and repeated at the end of their meal what Jesus did on that first night. This grew into what was later called 'The Eucharist' ('Thanksgiving') and later still 'Holy Communion' or 'The Mass'. Many Christians still call it 'The Lord's Supper.'

In this 'acted story' Jesus was committing himself again to God's way, the way of love and caring. He was prepared to face death, rather than go back on what he knew to be true about God his Father. He made his commitment by quoting some words from a poem of Jeremiah's; his death would make possible what Jeremiah had called 'the new covenant' – the new agreement between men and God, the agreement to which Jesus had been calling men and women when he appealed to them to 'change their ways' and 'trust in the Good News'.

Jesus had often used a feast or supper as a picture or symbol of the time when the world would be really God's family and God's purposes would all have been achieved. This last supper together would be for his friends a specially vivid symbol of that time, and of the cost of it – his own death.

He was, indeed, giving 'his very self'.

When supper was over, they all sang a hymn. It was almost certainly one of the psalms from what is called the 'Egypt Hallel' (Psalms 113–118). The word 'Hallel' means 'Praise (God)', and these particular psalms were to be sung at the Passover Festival* in praise to God for rescuing, long ago, his people from Egypt; this rescue was the theme of the Passover Festival. The words of these psalms must have meant much to Jesus, for he was offering his life to rescue people from all that hindered or stopped them from living together as God's family.

*There is some uncertainty over the exact point within the festival at which these events took place: Mark (14. 12–16), followed by Matthew (26. 17ff) and even more closely by Luke (21. 7–16), suggest that the supper was the actual Passover meal itself. John, on the other hand, seems to suggest (13.1, 18.28, 19.14) that the whole series of events took place *before* the Passover had actually started.

As Jesus went out of the upper room that night into the darkness, he went out to face the might of Rome and the authority of the Jewish government. He had nothing in his hands except his dedication to living in God's way and his love and care for people. He went out with those words of praise to God on his lips. This, for him, was the only kind of leadership that was real leadership; the leadership of a teacher, the leadership of a servant. This was the kind of leader God wanted him to be; he had settled that at those 'testings' in the desert at the very beginning. But it must have made no sense to anybody, even among his friends; it certainly did not to Judas Iscariot. He believed that Jesus must have got it wrong, somehow. But he had not.

There is an old poem which Jesus must have read in the Bible scrolls in Galilee, and perhaps read often. It was written in a deportation camp in Babylon nearly six hundred years before. It pictures the suffering of the Hebrew people, their defeat by the Babylonians, the destruction of Jerusalem, the scattering of its inhabitants. But it speaks of the Hebrew people as suffering on behalf of the whole world; their role in the history of the world was to be the world's teacher, not to be the world's conqueror; there was not to be a sort of Jewish Empire to take the place of the Babylonian Empire. Jesus agreed with that poem.

When he talked to his friends of what their work should be, he used words like these:
Again Jesus asked, 'What shall I compare the Kingdom of God with? It is like this. A woman takes some yeast and mixes it with forty litres of flour, until the whole batch of dough rises.'
(Luke 13.20–21)

'You are like salt for all mankind. But if salt loses its saltiness there is no way to make it salty again. It has become worthless, so it is thrown out and people trample on it.'
(Matthew 5.13)

This is far from what the religious leaders in Galilee, the freedom fighters or the Sadducees in Jerusalem thought the Jewish people should be. But Jesus believed it was God's way – and that was enough.

'Christ Mocked' by Hieronymus Bosch (1450-1516)

11

The execution of Jesus

When Jesus went out of the house into the darkness of the night, he went out to his arrest and execution. Jesus must have known that the end was near. His friends, to judge from their conversation at the supper table, were still living in a dream world.

The tragedy (as it must have seemed to everybody) was that Jesus, who had never made any claim to be God's chosen leader ('Messiah'), died as though he had, executed by the Roman governor as a rebel.

There seems to have been some trouble in the city that Passover. The two men between whom Jesus was soon to be crucified were not just 'bandits' but freedom fighters (though they were 'bandits' in the eyes of the Roman government); it seems that they had been guilty of some rioting in the streets. It was precisely because of the danger of such rioting that the governor, Pilate, came up from his headquarters in Caesarea to Jerusalem with his military escort to keep a check on the crowds who were up for the Festival. It was in this confused situation that Jesus met his death.

Here is the story of what happened as Luke told it, starting from the end of the supper.

Jesus left the city and went, as he usually did, to the Mount of Olives; and the disciples went with him. When he arrived at the place, he said to them, 'Pray that you will not fall into temptation.'

Then he went off from them about the distance of a stone's throw and knelt down and prayed. 'Father,' he said, 'if you will, take this cup of suffering away from me. Not my will, however, but your will be done.' An angel from heaven appeared to him and strengthened him. In great anguish he prayed even more fervently; his sweat was like drops of blood falling to the ground.

Rising from his prayer, he went back to the disciples and found them asleep, so great was their grief. And he said to them, 'Why are you sleeping? Get up and pray that you will not fall into temptation.'

Jesus was still speaking when a crowd arrived, led by Judas, one of the twelve disciples. He came up to Jesus to kiss him. But Jesus said, 'Judas, is it with a kiss that you betray the Son of Man?'

When the disciples who were with Jesus saw what was going to happen, they asked, 'Shall we use our swords, Lord?' And one of them struck the High Priest's slave and cut off his right ear. But Jesus said, 'Enough of this!' He touched the man's ear and healed him.

Then Jesus said to the chief priests and the officers of the Temple guard and the elders who had come there to get him, 'Did you have to come with swords and clubs, as though I were an outlaw? I was with you in the Temple every day, and you did not try to arrest me. But this is your hour to act, when the power of darkness rules.'

They arrested Jesus and took him away into the house of the High Priest; and Peter followed at a distance. A fire had been lit in the centre of the courtyard, and Peter joined those who were sitting round it. When one of the servant-girls saw him sitting there at the fire, she looked straight at him and said, 'This man too was with Jesus!' But Peter denied it: 'Woman, I don't even know him!'

After a little while a man noticed Peter and said, 'You are one of them, too!'

But Peter answered, 'Man, I am not!'

And about an hour later another man insisted strongly, 'There isn't any doubt that this man was with Jesus, because he also is a Galilean!'

But Peter answered, 'Man, I don't know what you are talking about!'

At once, while he was still speaking, a cock crowed. The Lord turned round and looked straight at Peter, and Peter remembered that the Lord had said to him, 'Before the cock crows tonight, you will say three times that you do not know me.' Peter went out and wept bitterly.

The men who were guarding Jesus mocked him and beat him. They blindfolded him and asked him, 'Who hit you? Guess!' And they said many other insulting things to him.

When day came, the elders, the chief priests, and the teachers of the Law met together, and Jesus was brought before the Council. 'Tell us,' they said, 'are you the Messiah?'

He answered, 'If I tell you, you will not believe me, and if I ask you a question you will not answer. But from now on the Son of Man will be seated on the right of Almighty God.' They all said, 'Are you, then, the Son of God?'

He answered them, 'You say that I am.' And they said, 'We don't need any witnesses! We ourselves have heard what he said!'

The whole group rose up and took Jesus before Pilate, where they began to accuse him: 'We caught this man misleading our people, telling them not to pay taxes to the Emperor and claiming that he himself is the Messiah, a king.' Pilate asked him, 'Are you the king of the Jews?'

'So you say,' answered Jesus. Then Pilate said to the chief priests and the crowds, 'I find no reason to condemn this man.'

But they insisted even more strongly, 'With his teaching he is starting a riot among the people all through Judea. He began in Galilee and now has come here.'

When Pilate heard this, he asked, 'Is this man a Galilean?' When he learnt that Jesus was from the region ruled by Herod, he sent him to Herod, who was also in Jerusalem at that time. Herod was very pleased when he saw Jesus, because he had heard about him and had been wanting to see him for a long time. He was hoping to see Jesus perform some miracle. So Herod asked Jesus many questions, but Jesus made no answer. The chief priests and the teachers of the Law stepped forward and made strong accusations against Jesus. Herod and his soldiers mocked Jesus and treated him with contempt; then they put a fine robe on him and sent him back to Pilate. On that very day Herod and Pilate became friends; before this they had been enemies.

Pilate called together the chief priests, the leaders, and the people, and said to them, 'You brought this man to me and said that he was misleading the people. Now, I have examined him here in your presence, and I have not found him guilty of any of the crimes you accuse him of. Nor did Herod find him guilty, for he sent him back to us. There is nothing this man has done to deserve death. So I will have him whipped and let him go.' (At each Passover Feast Pilate had to set free one prisoner for them.)

The whole crowd cried out, 'Kill him! Set Barabbas free for us!' (Barabbas had been put in prison for a riot that had taken place in the city, and for murder.)

Pilate wanted to set Jesus free, so he appealed to the crowd again. But they shouted back, 'Crucify him! Crucify him!'

Pilate said to them the third time, 'But what crime has he committed? I cannot find anything he has done to deserve death! I will have him whipped and set him free.'

But they kept on shouting at the top of their voices that Jesus should be crucified, and finally their shouting succeeded. So Pilate passed the sentence on Jesus that they were asking for. He set free the man they wanted, the one who had been put in prison for riot and murder, and he handed Jesus over for them to do as they wished.

The soldiers took Jesus away and as they were going, they met a man from Cyrene named Simon, who was coming into the city from the country. They seized him, put the cross on him and made him carry it behind Jesus.

A large crowd of people followed him; among them were some women who were weeping and wailing for him. Jesus turned to them and said, 'Women of Jerusalem! Don't cry for me, but for yourselves and your children. For the days are coming when people will say, "How lucky are the women who never had children, who never bore babies, who never nursed them!" That will be the time when people will say to the mountains, "Fall on us!" and to the hills, "Hide us!" For if such things as these are done when the wood is green, what will happen when it is dry?'

Two other men, both of them criminals, were also led out to be put to death with Jesus. When they came to the place called 'The Skull', they crucified Jesus there, and the two criminals, one on his right and the other on his left. Jesus said, 'Forgive them, Father! They don't know what they are doing.'

They divided his clothes among themselves by throwing dice. The people stood there watching, while the Jewish leaders jeered at him: 'He saved others; let him save himself, if he is the Messiah whom God has chosen!'

The soldiers also mocked him: they came up to him and offered him cheap wine, and said, 'Save yourself if you are the king of the Jews!' Above him were written these words: 'This is the King of the Jews.'

One of the criminals hanging there hurled insults at him: 'Aren't you the Messiah? Save yourself and us!'

The other one, however, rebuked him, saying, 'Don't you fear God? You received the same sentence he did. Ours, however, is only right, because we are getting what we deserve for what we did; but he has done no wrong.' And he said to Jesus, 'Remember me, Jesus, when you come as King!'

Jesus said to him, 'I promise you that today you will be in Paradise with me.'

It was about twelve o'clock when the sun stopped shining and darkness covered the whole country until three o'clock' and the curtain hanging in the Temple was torn in two. Jesus cried out in a loud voice, 'Father! In your hands I place my spirit!' He said this and died.

The army officer saw what had happened, and he praised God, saying, 'Certainly he was a good man!'

When the people who had gathered there to watch the spectacle saw what happened, they all went back home, beating their breasts in sorrow. All those who knew Jesus personally, including the women who had followed him from Galilee, stood at a distance to watch.
(Luke 22.39–23.49)

We cannot expect to reconstruct a more detailed account than this of what actually happened. But some things need commenting on.

The first is this. The accounts we have in the Gospels were not simply written down as a detailed historical account of the last events in the life of Jesus. They are all accounts of how Jesus died which were recited or read as part of later Christian worship. They were written to bring home to all Christians, as they worshipped together, the great cost which had been paid for their freedom; Jesus' love of people and love for them had taken him to his death. In the love of Jesus they saw the love of God; it was God's love and God's way that, day in and day out, he had tried to make clear in what he said and what he did. This is what mattered to him; and he would not go back on it when his very life was at stake. So we must read the accounts of the execution of Jesus in the gospels as a picture of what the terrible death of Jesus came to mean, later on, to his friends.

Remember, too, that crucifixion was the Roman method of executing criminals and slaves and especially rebels. It was usually a long and lingering death from thirst and starvation; the condemned man was exposed as a public spectacle to the crowds, and he was at the mercy of carrion birds. He could linger for days. Many crucifixions had taken place in Judea and Galilee; and nobody in Palestine was in any doubt of how terrifying such a death was. When Jesus talked about being ready to 'carry a cross', it would sound worse in Jewish ears than 'facing a firing squad' sounds to us.

The second thing to notice is this. At the time the Gospels were written, the Christians and the Jews had become very bitter against one another. The Christians, when they talked about Jesus' execution, tended to blame the Jews and let the Romans off much more lightly. But the truth is probably much more equally balanced.

The leading members of the Great Council in Jerusalem – the Jewish body that had official dealings with the Roman governor – were certainly scared about Jesus and took him seriously. When they learned from Judas that Jesus was in the city again, they got him to take them to him, somewhere away from the crowds. The Temple police seemed to have been accompanied by a detachment of Roman soldiers – perhaps the Jewish authorities had already warned Pilate that a dangerous rebel was in the city. The members of the Council did not sleep much that night. They seemed to have met before dawn to prepare a case to put before Pilate. They decided to charge Jesus with claiming to be the Jewish king and plotting against Rome. They probably believed that this was true of Jesus – they must have received many alarming reports. And it was as a threat to the Roman peace that Jesus was finally condemned by the Roman governor – Pilate put the death-charge 'Jewish king' on the cross. Jesus had indeed made a bid for the leadership of the Jewish people; and because that was what God had called him to do, he had put it to the proof finally in the capital city and challenged the power of the government itself. And though the leadership he sought was far from what the freedom-fighters were wanting, it could easily be made to look as if he were in fact a rebel against Rome, especially as when at his arrest some of his friends proved to be armed. And there was only one fate for any rebel against Rome – crucifixion.

The members of the Great Council in Jerusalem who brought Jesus to Pilate for trial must clearly bear some responsibility for his death. So must Pilate himself. But what about Judas? What responsibility must he bear?

Why did he betray Jesus in the first place? We do not *know* his reasons; we can only guess. Perhaps he was a dogmatic man with fixed ideas and still believed, as others did, that Jesus was indeed God's Chosen Leader sent to establish a Jewish Empire. 'Perhaps,' he may have thought, 'if I force his hand and put him in a situation where he has got to act, he will show himself as the Chosen Leader everybody expects and then God will come and destroy the Romans.' He could not understand why Jesus was taking such a 'soft' line. So he put Jesus into a dangerous situation. But Jesus did nothing – and God did nothing. When Judas realised the terrible mistake he had made, and that Jesus was about to be executed as a result of his action, he went out and committed suicide.

By Friday afternoon, Jesus too was dead; and before the beginning of the Feast late on Friday evening, he had been buried in an obscure grave.

12

Was this the end?

Jesus' friends were scared and frightened. Despite everything he had told them, they had never expected an execution like this. They were taken completely by surprise. Both their courage and their loyalty broke down.

Jesus, as we have seen, had spoken again and again about the sort of work he believed God had given him to do. It had nothing to do with the convictions of the freedom-fighters, and it was very different from what the religious leaders, like the Pharisees, hoped. But his friends were so set in their minds and Jesus was so radical and beyond them that even on the last night, so Luke tells us, they were still arguing about their public positions 'when Jesus became king'. Others besides Judas probably believed God would himself come and make Jesus a conqueror of the Romans. Luke tells us a story about two of his friends going home after it was all over and saying "And we had hoped that he would be the one who was going to set Israel free!" (Luke 24.21)

No wonder they were thrown into confusion.

One report tells us that they hid in a room with locked doors. They were frightened in case the soldiers decided to round them up too. It was a black weekend for them all.

Here is what Mark tells us happened after Jesus died – quite quickly for such a death.

It was towards evening when Joseph of Arimathea arrived. He was a respected member of the Council, who was waiting for the coming of the Kingdom of God. It was Preparation day (that is, the day before the Sabbath), so Joseph went boldly into the presence of Pilate and asked him for the body of Jesus. Pilate was surprised to hear that Jesus was already dead. He called the army officer and asked him if Jesus had been dead a long time. After hearing the officer's report, Pilate told Joseph he could have the body. Joseph brought a linen sheet, took the body down, wrapped it in the sheet and placed it in a tomb which had been dug out of solid rock. Then he rolled a large stone across the entrance to the tomb. Mary Magdalene and Mary the mother of Jesus were watching, and saw where the body of Jesus was placed.

(Mark 15.42–47)

It was all over – or so it seemed.

PART II

The Tapestry, Coventry Cathedral (Graham Sutherland, 1957)

1

'Jesus lives!'

For the friends of Jesus, in the hours following his death, life was cruelly disappointing. They had thought that Jesus was God's Chosen One (had not Peter called him 'Messiah'?), but the man of whom they had had such high hopes had been tortured and killed. They had expected the future to be gloriously happy, but their leader lay dead in a borrowed tomb. They had believed that their country was to be set free, but it was still as much enslaved as ever. Their future was barren. Perhaps their friend had misled them; perhaps he hadn't known God as well as he had claimed; perhaps he had got it all wrong. In bitterness and grief they met and comforted each other as best they could.

Yet it was from that group of bewildered friends that a movement sprang which was to change the world. A movement which, 1950 years later, has over 900 million followers. How did the movement begin? What was it about its leader that was so extraordinary that his influence lives on? It is partly to try to answer these questions that this book has been written. But before we explore any further the views of his earliest followers, let's see what people today make of Jesus. If we can see what makes him important today we may be able to discover some of the things which made him so important to his first friends.

Suppose you were to conduct a poll of Christians now and asked them 'Why is Jesus important to you?' you would probably get a variety of answers. Some would say, 'Because he shows me how to live', others might reply, 'Because he teaches me what God is really like' and yet others might tell you, 'Because he shows me what love and goodness are'. Not all these answers are exactly alike, which is not surprising, for everyone seems to see Jesus slightly differently. If you were to continue your poll by asking another question: 'What one word or phrase best describes Jesus?', you would find just as much variety in the answers – 'Son of God'; 'Saviour'; 'King'; 'The Man for Others'; 'Love in action'; 'The Human Face of God'.

Of course there are also people today who do not approve of Jesus. Many orthodox Jews still think of him as a heretic and blasphemer. Many other people, from all sorts of backgrounds, dismiss him as a misguided fanatic whose teaching was quite impractical. Some go as far as claiming that the influence of his teaching has been actually harmful! This wide range of views about Jesus is nothing new. During his lifetime, and especially in the period just following his crucifixion, disagreement about him was so violent that it was literally a matter of life and death. His opponents felt so strongly about him that they were prepared to kill those who supported him. His friends felt so strongly about him that they were prepared to die rather than change their views.

In fact, the first person to be put to death because of his loyalty to Jesus was a Greek-speaking Jew called Stephen. He was stoned by a mob which was under the direction of another Greek-speaking Jew called Saul, who later changed his mind completely about Jesus and became one of the leading figures amongst his followers, only to be put to death in his turn about thirty years later.

People's feelings about Jesus remain equally divided today. In some parts of the world Christians are imprisoned and killed because of their beliefs (Archbishop Romero in El Salvador is a recent example), and yet this treatment does not seem to curb people's loyalty to or interest in Jesus. He remains as fascinating as ever. For example, a survey of young people in Britain in the late 1970s showed that just over one third of them believed that Jesus was 'God in human form' while almost another third believed that he was a 'prophet' or a 'good teacher'. Jesus is not forgotten nor thought of as irrelevant. People still find themselves challenged to make up their minds about him.

When you are trying to find the answer to a problem, you often have to ask a lot of questions to help you 'make up your mind'. In the second part of this book we try to set out the questions to which you need to find answers when trying to make up your mind about Jesus. We have also tried to show the sort of evidence which is available to help you find those answers. Most of the questions, and therefore most of the evidence, could be described as 'historical', but there comes a point, as we shall see, at which the question of Jesus ceases to be simply the sort of question which a historian could be expected to answer. This is why it is such an important question.

2

Did Jesus really exist?

Part I of this book ended with an account of the trial and execution of Jesus. You might have expected that Part II would begin with a discussion of the event known as the Resurrection. In fact we want to leave that subject until the very end of this section. Meanwhile there are a number of other important questions which need answering before we go any further.

One of the questions commonly asked about Jesus is absolutely basic – and it's this: 'Did Jesus really exist?' Fortunately it's reasonably easy to answer.

The best answer, apart from the evidence of the New Testament itself, is the fact that in the early days it did not occur to even the fiercest opponent of Christianity to doubt the actual existence of Jesus. Apart from that piece of 'negative' evidence, the most famous evidence in support of Jesus' existence comes from a Roman writer called Tacitus. In his *Annals*, which were composed soon after AD 110, Tacitus was telling how Nero met the charge of having been responsible for burning down much of the city of Rome. We read:

> Now in order to put down the rumour Nero contrived to produce culprits to whom he meted out the direst punishments; these were the people – detested enough already because of all manner of abominable deeds – whom the populace called 'Chrestians'. The name has to do with one 'Christus' whom the procurator Pontius Pilate had caused to be executed during the reign of Tiberius . . .   (XV,44)

It is interesting to note that in this quotation Tacitus does not know the name 'Jesus' at all and thinks that 'Christus' is a proper name. A similar mistake seems to have been made in his use of the word 'Chrestians', but this is easily explained – Chrestus was a familiar and common Roman name.

Apart from the *Annals*, the only other piece of Roman evidence comes from Suetonius, in his work *The Lives of the Caesars*. This was written later than Tacitus, but in it we find this: 'The Jews . . . who under the instigation of Chrestus were constantly creating disturbances, Claudius expelled from Rome.' If you assume that Suetonius made the same error as Tacitus in calling Christ 'Chrestus', then this may be an account of the problems caused by the intrusion of Christianity into the Jewish community in Rome.

There are two other sources outside the New Testament to which we can look for independent witnesses. The first is Josephus; the second the Talmud. Let us deal with Josephus first.

Josephus was a Jewish historian writing in Rome between AD 75 and 90. In his work *The Antiquities of the Jews* he mentions the stoning of 'the brother of Jesus the so-called Christ, whose name was James' (XX.9.1). Earlier in the work (XVIII.3.3) we find a passage describing the troubles during Pontius Pilate's term of office. Although the text at this point seems to have been tampered with fairly early on when the manuscripts were being copied out by hand, it looks as if Josephus had at least the following to say about Jesus:

> And there arose about this time one Jesus . . . who led away many Jews, and also many of the Greeks. This man was the so-called Christ. And when Pilate had condemned him to the cross when he had been accused by the chief men among us, those who had followed him at first did not cease . . . and even now the tribe of Christians, so named after him, has not yet died out.

The other independent source of information is the Talmud – a collection of Jewish traditions which arose over the centuries. This contains a few references to Jesus, e.g. that he was a magician who was hanged on the day of preparation for Passover (Babylonian Talmud: Tractate Sanhedrin 43a).

There are, however, many other references to Jesus which are not only outside the books of the New Testament but are also outside the conventional historical writings of the time. Here is an example:

> Jesus says: 'Wherever there are two they are not without God, and where one is alone, I say, I am with him.
>> Lift up the stone
>> and there thou wilt find me;
>> cleave the wood
>> and I am there.'

This quotation comes from a book known as the Gospel of Thomas (written in about AD 140).

During the growth of the early Church there developed a large number of different sects on the fringe of the Church, which were later labelled as 'Gnostic' (the Greek work 'Gnosis' means 'knowledge'), because they placed great emphasis upon 'knowledge' as the means to salvation. This 'knowledge' was often of a mysterious and secret nature – and each of the sects claimed that it alone possessed the true knowledge. An example may help to illustrate the point.

Amongst other things, Gnostics were very concerned about the afterlife. They thought that the soul, on its ascent from earth to heaven, would need a password when it came face to face with the cosmic spirits who might bar its way. In the following passage the password is revealed by Jesus himself.

> The Lord revealed unto me what the soul must say as it goeth up to heaven and how it must answer each of the powers above. 'I have taken knowledge of myself and have gathered myself together out of every quarter and have not sown children unto the Ruler but have rooted out his roots and gathered together the members that were scattered abroad and I know thee who thou art for I belong to the higher powers.'
>
> (Greek Gospel of Philip)

Most of these Gnostic writings are obviously not authentic accounts of Jesus' life or teaching. They do, however, in an indirect way, offer further evidence of the fact that a well-known teacher called Jesus had lived in Palestine in the first century AD. If one adds to this the writings of Tacitus, Suetonius and Josephus, and the traditions of the Talmud, one has enough evidence to lay alongside the New Testament material and so build up a convincing case for Jesus having actually existed and having been put to death by Pilate as a potential troublemaker, despite the honour in which he was held by his followers.

Crucifixion, Birmingham Cathedral (Peter Eugene Ball, 1983)

3

What are the sources of our detailed information about Jesus?

Following Jesus' death there was a remarkable and unexpected growth in the number of his followers. They talked enthusiastically about Jesus having been raised from the dead and they experienced a power which they claimed was the Holy Spirit coming upon them. As a result of their teaching and preaching new fellowships came into existence and these too claimed a deep awareness of the risen Jesus amongst them.

How do we know all this? Much of our evidence comes from 'The Acts of the Apostles', a book which deals with the period of time immediately following Jesus' death and which gives us some indication of how Jesus' teachings were passed on. It is one of the most important documents we have about this period – and so we ought to look at it carefully to see how reliable it is.

Normally when you read a book and try to decide what kind of book it is, you look at its title and you look at the name of the author. For example, if you turn to the title-page of this book you will see at once who wrote it (though in fact it won't tell you which author wrote which bits) and the name and address of the publisher; inside the front cover, more information is given – the name of the copyright-holders, the year it was published, and so on.

Unfortunately we have none of this kind of information for the 'Acts of the Apostles'. We do not know who published it. We do not know exactly when it was written. It's not even absolutely certain who wrote it, although must scholars are agreed that it was a man called Luke. Why do they believe this to be the case? There are three clues.

First, some parts of the book are like a travel-diary – 'We left by ship from Troas and sailed straight across to Samothrace' (cf Acts 16.10–17; 20.15–21.8; 27.1–28.16), which suggests that the author was actually with Paul on parts of the journey. Secondly, it is equally likely that he was not far away when Paul was in prison in Caesarea and he may have stayed with Paul when he eventually reached Rome. The person who best fits in with both these facts is Luke, whom Paul refers to in his letters (e.g. in Col 4.14) as 'Luke our dear doctor'. The third clue is found in the opening sentences of 'Acts': 'In my first book, dear Theophilus, I wrote about all the things that Jesus did and taught . . .'. The name 'Theophilus' is also found in the first verses of Luke's gospel. This all suggests that Luke, a well-educated doctor, wrote both Acts and the gospel which bears his name.

This is where archaeology also helps us, because it supports the accuracy of his observations. His account of Paul's travels and eventual arrest seems to be as reliable a document as any, Christian or non-Christian, which has come down to us from that time.

It would seem, then, that we can look to Acts as a reasonably reliable book. Now one of the interesting points which comes out in Acts is that at an early stage the followers of Jesus appealed to words he was believed to have used, and used them as authoritative teaching. Here is an example from Acts 11.16. Peter is involved in an argument with the other apostles about the gift of the Holy Spirit. As part of his case Peter quotes Jesus: 'Then I remembered what the Lord had said: "John baptised with water but you will be baptised with the Holy Spirit".' (cf Acts 1.5 and Luke 3.16.) There is a similar example in Acts 20.35: Paul is speaking to the Christians in Ephesus and reminds them of Jesus' moral teaching – 'I have shown you in all things that by working hard in this way we must help the weak, remembering the words that the Lord Jesus himself said: "There is more happiness in giving than in receiving".'

All this suggests that among Christians great importance was attached to what Jesus had said, and that his words were remembered and handed on. The same was true of the story of Jesus' life. In Acts 10.38 we read this: 'You know about Jesus of Nazareth, how God poured out on him the Holy Spirit and power. He went everywhere, doing good and healing all who were under the power of the Devil, for God was with him.' There are many passages similar to this, throughout the book.

What we seem to have established, then, is this – that Acts is a reliable book, and that in that book there are many examples of the words and actions of Jesus being remembered and referred to by his earliest followers.

But now we hit on a real problem. As far as we can tell, Jesus himself wrote down nothing of his own teachings. He had used poems and parables – and these had been remembered by his followers. After his death, these were passed on by word of mouth. It was not for some years after the crucifixion that the words were systematically written down. Why did this happen? It was an astonishingly important development in the life of the early Church – so what was it that caused the change from the spoken to the written word?

The answer seems to be this. Quite apart from the fact that Jesus' very first followers expected him to return in power and judgement soon after his death, they were in any case only a small group who had been with him during his life and knew each other well. So there was no need to write anything down. But the movement spread rapidly – helped on its way by some fierce persecution from the Jewish authorities who were opposed to the new teachings about Jesus. Although all his followers at this time were Jews from Jerusalem or Galilee or nearby, within a few years some of them had moved away from Palestine altogether and settled in places like Cyprus and northern Syria.

Being so far from Jerusalem, which was still the centre of the Christian movement, these Jewish Christians found it difficult to observe their traditional customs. Indeed the new movement was so popular that non-Jews (Gentiles) wanted to join as well. The earliest known Christian piece of writing refers to this very problem. It is mentioned in Acts and is a letter taken by Paul and Barnabas from a meeting of the 'Twelve' in Jerusalem to a new 'church' (as meetings of Christ's followers were called) in Antioch. (See Acts 15.23–29.)

So the rapid expansion of the movement meant that Jesus' teachings were being heard by people who had neither met him nor understood his Jewish background. Because they had not had the same tradition of memorisation as their Jewish fellow-Christians, and because they needed to know more about the person of Jesus, the pressures would have been on for someone to start writing things down. It must be remembered too that Ephesus and Rome were the great writing and publishing centres of the Mediterranean. The movement of Christianity to these places would inevitably have led to thought being given to the written publication of the Christian message.

It also became clear that the 'Twelve' could not hope to travel around all the new churches. Indeed, as those first disciples died one by one there was a more urgent need for the story to be told in a permanent and authentic fashion – especially as the earlier hopes of Jesus' speedy return had clearly not materialised.

All of these things – expansion into the Gentile world, persecution and the deaths of the original followers – meant that written material instead of spoken messages was required.

Now this may have given you the impression that the growth of the churches and the way documents came to be written was an orderly and controlled affair. Nothing of the sort – as in any other rapidly expanding organisation, things happened in a variety of ways. 'Epistles' were written to keep the new fellowships in touch with the centre, to provide them with guidelines for the development of their faith. For a variety of reasons and in different places four writers composed documents known as 'Gospels' – and, as it happens, in doing so invented a totally new literary form. All this took place over a short period of time – approximately sixty or seventy years at most – a time which was extraordinarily creative.

In answer to the question at the beginning of this chapter we can therefore say this. After Jesus' death his followers preserved and communicated his teaching, as he had done, by word of mouth, but as the Christian movement spread, there developed a need for the written word and this gave rise to the documents which now form the New Testament. Almost two thousand years later it is those self-same documents which are the prime source for our detailed knowledge about Jesus. We shall need to look at them with close attention if we are to reach a fuller understanding of him and his message.

But first we need to trace in a little more detail the process which preceded the actual writing down of the material. This happened in two stages.

4

How was the teaching of Jesus first passed on?

We have seen in the 'Acts' that Jesus' sayings were indeed remembered by his followers and were used by them to help solve some of the new problems which they faced. But we also know that Acts was written a number of years after the events it describes. Luke probably did not finish writing Acts until AD 60 and the very earliest he could have started it was AD 56. (We know the AD 60 date because it corresponds with events described in the final chapter). Can we then discover any other sayings of Jesus, recorded by his followers, which come from a period before AD 60? The answer is 'Yes, we can'.

In AD 49 Paul wrote from Corinth to a group of converts in Thessalonica (in Northern Greece). His letter contains the phrase 'You yourselves know very well that the Day of the Lord will come as a thief comes at night' (1 Thessalonians 5.2). This is an echo of a saying of Jesus in Luke 12.39:
> 'And you can be sure that if the owner of a house knew the time when the thief would come, he would not let the thief break into his house. And you too must be ready, because the Son of Man will come at an hour when you are not expecting him.'

Look again at Paul's phrase: 'You yourselves know well . . .'. How could they 'know well', for they certainly did not have Luke's gospel in front of them? Paul himself supplies the answer; earlier in the letter he had written as follows:
> And now we beg and urge you in the name of the Lord Jesus to do even more. For you know the instructions we gave you by the authority of the Lord Jesus . . .
>
> (1 Thessalonians 4.1–2)

It is clear that Paul had taught them a number of Jesus' sayings. He in his turn had learnt them from some of the original disciples (see Corinthians 15.3, quoted below). But how had the disciples remembered them in the first place?

Jesus, following the practice of his day, used stories and poems to convey his message. These poems and rhyming sayings may not always be obvious in an English translation, but if you go back through the Greek, in which the stories were first written, to Aramaic, the language actually spoken by Jesus, you will discover strong rhythms and a sort of rhyming system which could help even the weakest memory to hold on to what was being said. So the material lent itself to easy memorisation. But the ability of the Christians to memorise Jesus' words also lay, to some extent, in their worship.

When the early Christian groups met for worship each Sunday, they would hear certain material in the form of hymns and prayers and these would be repeated regularly. They may well have had a primitive creed, that is, a summary of their beliefs, which they would recite. For example, in Paul's first letter to the church at Corinth (I Corinthians 15.3–5) he says this:

> I passed on to you what I received, which is of the greatest importance: that Christ died for our sins, as written in the Scriptures; that he was buried and that he was raised to life three days later, as written in the Scriptures: that he appeared to Peter and then to all twelve apostles.

It could well be that that statement made by Paul was a creed he had been taught.

As well as hymns, prayers and creeds, the regular worshipper would hear stories and sayings retold by the senior members of the congregation.

Other stories and sayings would be used at the other fairly frequent ceremonies like baptism – and we can imagine that there would have been regular instruction for new converts, when the teachings of the new faith would be passed on by those who had themselves remembered the words of Christ.

Amongst all this teaching there would have been certain key stories, for example those connected with the Last Supper and the Crucifixion, and these by repetition would become part of their common stock of knowledge. It is interesting to note that in the case of the Last Supper story there were further aids to memorisation. Not only were the words of Jesus remembered, but so were his actions. Bread was broken and shared and wine was drunk as a way of re-enacting and re-presenting what Jesus had done.

In the rapidly expanding Christian movement, however, it was inevitable that from one place to another there would be variations in the way the sayings and stories were remembered. A fascinating example of this* can be found in the same letter of Paul to the Corinthians. He is describing the Last Supper:

> For I received from the Lord the teaching that I passed on to you: that the Lord Jesus, on the night he was betrayed, took a piece of bread, gave thanks to God, broke it and said, 'This is my body, which is for you. Do this in memory of me.' In the same way, after supper he took the cup and said, 'This cup is God's new covenant, sealed with my blood. Whenever you drink it, do so in memory of me'. (I Corinthians 11.23–25)

Paul wrote this some twenty years after the event he is describing, and already the way he has quoted Jesus suggests a formula used by the Christians in their worship. We can compare his version with those found in Mark 14.22–25 (cf Matthew 26.26–29) and Luke 22.15–20.

---

*You will remember that this account and the following one from Mark's gospel were quoted in Part I of this book, on p44, but it is such an important example that it is set out in full again here.

Mark 14.22–25
While they were eating, Jesus took
the bread, gave a prayer of thanks,
broke it, and gave it to them.
'Take it,' he said, 'this is
my body.'

Then he took
the cup, gave thanks to God, and
handed it to them; and they all
drank from it. Jesus said: 'This is
my blood which is poured out for many,
my blood which seals God's covenant.
I assure you, I will never again drink
the new wine in the Kingdom of God.'

Luke 22.15–20
And he said to them: 'I have wanted
so much to eat this Passover meal
with you before I suffer! For I
tell you, I will never eat it until
it is given its real meaning in the
Kingdom of God.'

Then Jesus picked up
the cup, gave thanks to God and
said, 'Take this and share it among
yourselves;

for I tell you that I will
not drink this wine from now on
until the Kingdom of God comes.'
Then he took the bread, gave thanks
to God, broke it, and gave it to them,
saying 'This is my body'.

If you compare these three versions you will see that there are some major differences between them. How did such a variety of versions arise?

We can assume that the early Christians met in small groups throughout the Eastern Mediterranean area and, as part of their worship, remembered and used the story of the 'Last Supper'. They seem to have had a basic outline but within that outline to have used a variety of words. Now that was a process which also happened to other stories. For example, compare these two passages:

Mark 2.18–20
On one occasion the followers of
John the Baptist and the Pharisees
were fasting. Some people came to
Jesus and asked him 'Why is it that
the disciples of John the Baptist and
the disciples of the Pharisees fast, but
yours do not?' Jesus answered: 'Do
you expect the guests at a wedding
party to go without food? Of course
not! As long as the bridegroom is with
them they can not do that. But the
days will come when the bridegroom
will be taken away from them;
and then on that day they
will go without food.'

Luke 5.33–35

A group of people said to him, 'The
disciples of John fast frequently and
offer up prayers, and the disciples of
the Pharisees do the same, but yours
eat and drink'. The Jesus said to them:
'Do you think you can make the guests at
a wedding party go without food?

But the
days will come, and when the bridegroom
will be taken away from them
then in those days they
will go without food.'

(The translation of Luke's version reads rather awkwardly here, but the words and phrases have been specially chosen to show exactly where Luke's Greek ran parallel with Mark's Greek, and exactly where and by how much, the two versions differed.)

You can see that both stories begin with slightly different attempts to set the scene, and even after that the wording continues to be slightly different – but, notice the punchline, the climax at the end ('But the days will come when the bridegroom will be taken away from them . . .'). In both versions the punch-line is the same or almost so. If you compare other stories in the Gospels you will see that this is often the case. The scene-setting varies, but the climax remains the same.

It is worth noticing, though, that in some cases it looks as though the punch-line was circulating quite separately on its own for some time before becoming attached to a story. We can tell this because sometimes the same sayings become attached to more than one story. Compare, for example, these two passages:

Matthew 19.27–30
Then Peter spoke up. 'Look,' he said,
'we have left everything and followed
you. What will we have?' Jesus said
to them: 'I tell you this: when the
Son of Man sits on his glorious throne
in the New Age, then you twelve followers
of mine will also sit on thrones to
judge the twelve tribes of Israel.
And everyone who has left houses or
brothers or sisters or father or mother
or children or fields for my sake
will be receiving much
more and will be given
eternal life.
But many who now are first will be last,
and many who now are last will be first.'

Luke 18.28–29
Then Peter said, 'Look! We have
left our homes to follow you.'
He said
to them, 'I tell you this:

anyone who leaves home or wife
or brothers or parents
or children for the sake of the
Kingdom of God will receive much
more in the present age, and eternal
life in the age to come.'

Matthew's version, as you see, ends with the words 'But many who now are first will be last, and many who now are last will be first'. Luke's version does not have those words, but he actually does record them elsewhere in his gospel (Luke 13.22–30) and attaches them to another story.

All this evidence seems to suggest very strongly that Jesus' teachings (and stories about him) were passed on initially by word of mouth, but that the contexts in which they were used – especially in worship and in instruction – created a fixed framework within which the material was able to retain a reasonably constant shape, even if the details of the wording varied from place to place.

It is important to remember that the evidence available to us is of two sorts. First of all, there is what we can discover from the Acts and the epistles about the way in which Jesus' teaching was used. Secondly there is the evidence of the gospels themselves – the fact that they contain different versions of what is clearly the same basic material. Any explanation of this fact, however, must account equally for the differences as for the similarities, and equally for the similarities as for the differences. Neither the one nor the other can be ignored.

5

How was the teaching of Jesus developed?

As we have seen, some of the differences between various versions of the same basic material could have come about simply as a result of different styles of different story-tellers (or indeed because of different translations from the original Aramaic, the language used by Jesus and the first disciples). But some differences seem to have arisen as the early Church struggled to meet changes in its circumstances, especially as relationships with the secular authorities (both Jewish and Roman) shifted and altered.

The problem facing the Church was this. Not only had Jesus and the first disciples spoken Aramaic, the common language of the Jewish people; all Jesus' teaching was set against the background of Jewish ideas, Jewish beliefs, Jewish practices. And then all the earliest followers of Jesus were Jews, and the message about Jesus was proclaimed in Jewish places of worship. But very soon Gentiles, such as Cornelius and his family (Acts 10), were asking to join the Church, and it was not long before there were some groups of disciples among whom the majority were Gentiles, living within Gentile communities. How were these Gentiles expected to behave when they became Christians? Should they continue to behave as their Gentile neighbours behaved? Should they, for example, still show loyalty to the Roman authorities and follow the Roman law, or were they now to follow the Jewish law, as all the disciples so far had done?

One example of this sort of problem – one which faced these new Gentile Christians almost every day – was the question of buying meat in the market place. There was always a chance that this meat had come from animals which had been sacrificed in the local pagan temple. No Jew (Christian or otherwise) would ever eat this meat. Should Gentiles who became Christians follow Jewish practice here or not? The Church was at first strongly divided on this issue. Paul's letters, for example, keep coming back to the matter. Paul himself clearly believed that Gentile Christians should not be bound by Jewish law – this would have been the opposite of the freedom which he believed Jesus had brought to the world. But it is equally clear, both from his letters and from Acts, that many of the Jewish Christians disagreed profoundly with Paul's point of view.

One of the reasons for this disagreement was the fact that Jesus had never spoken directly about this subject. The question just had not arisen amongst those amongst whom he had lived and taught. The Church leaders had therefore to look very carefully at what he *had* said, to see if there was anything which was in any way relevant. Some pieces of teaching appear to have been adapted specially to meet this problem, the most obvious case being the passage in Mark 7.14–19:

> Then Jesus called the crowd to him once more and said to them. 'Listen to me, all of you, and understand. There is nothing that goes into a person from the outside which can make him ritually unclean. Rather, it is what comes out of a person which makes him unclean.' When he left the crowd and went into the house, his disciples asked him to explain this saying. 'You are no more intelligent than the others,' Jesus said to them. 'Don't you understand? Nothing that goes into a person from the outside can really make him unclean, because it does not go into his heart but into his stomach and then goes on out of the body.' (In saying this, Jesus declared that all foods are fit to be eaten.)

We do not know who added that last phrase in brackets, but it obviously was not part of the original teaching, as the rest of the passage makes clear.

Another problem facing Gentile Christians in particular was the question of faithfulness between husband and wife. It was not just the simple question of whether divorce was allowed among Christians or not. That was, at least at first sight, fairly straightforward. Writing to the group of Christians at Corinth on this matter, Paul was able to refer directly to Jesus' teaching:

> For married people I have a command which is not my own but the Lord's: a wife must not leave her husband; but if she does, she must remain single or else be reconciled to her husband; and a husband must not divorce his wife.' (I Corinthians 7.10–11)

This is an obvious reference to the kind of teaching found in Mark's gospel:

> He said to them, 'A man who divorces his wife and marries another woman commits adultery against his wife. In the same way, a woman who divorces her husband and marries another man commits adultery.' (Mark 10.11–12)

However, there was a particular problem which Paul was having to deal with in Corinth on which Jesus had *not* given any guidance. This was the problem of a marriage where one partner had become a Christian and the other had not. In this new situation Paul could only preface his advice with the words 'I say, (I myself, not the Lord) . . .' and, interestingly, his advice seemed to make an exception to the general rule he had just quoted from Jesus.

In terms of general attitudes to the authorities, as opposed to specific questions of behaviour, there were phrases of Jesus which were clearly relevant. You will remember the story about Jesus which explained his attitude to Rome: 'Pay the Emperor what belongs to the Emperor, and pay God what belongs to God' (Matthew 22.21). That stood as a general rule for Christians wherever they lived. But Jesus' attitude to the Jews was the source of further problems for those Christians who continued to live in the Jewish-dominated areas of Palestine. Although Jesus had been unsparing in his criticism of the hypocrisy which he had found among some of the religious leaders of his day, his attitude to his fellow countrymen as a whole was one more of sorrow than of condemnation:

Matthew 23.37–39	Luke 13.34–35
'Jerusalem, Jerusalem! You kill the prophets and stone the messengers God has sent you! How many times have I wanted to put my arms around all your people, just as a hen gathers her chicks under her wings, but you would not let me! And so your Temple will be abandoned and empty. From now on, I tell you, you will never see me again until you say, "God bless him who comes in the name of the Lord." '	'Jerusalem, Jerusalem! You kill the prophets, you stone the messengers God has sent you! How many times have I wanted to put my arms round all your people, just as a hen gathers her chicks under her wings, but you would not let me! And so your Temple will be abandoned. I assure you that you will not see me until the time comes when you say "God bless him who comes in the name of the Lord." '

But relations between the Jewish authorities and the young Church seem to have grown progressively worse over the years, and this may well have affected some of the material preserved by the Church during the period before the gospels were written down.

A very striking example of this can be found in the story of the vineyard. This is one of the few stories told by Jesus which appear in more than two gospels. But in this particular case the story is also found outside the New Testament altogether, in an apocryphal book called the Gospel of Thomas. Here is the story as it appears in that source:

He said: 'A good man had a vineyard. He gave it to husbandmen that they might work it, and he received its fruit at their hand. He sent his servant that the husbandmen might give him fruit of the vineyard. They seized his servant, they beat him and all but killed him. The servant came and told his master. His master said "Perhaps they did not know him." He sent another servant; the husbandmen beat this other also. Then the master sent his son. He said "Perhaps they will reverence my son." Those husbandmen, since they knew that he was the heir of the vineyard, seized him and killed him. He that hath ears, let him hear.'

It is instructive to compare this version in some detail with the versions given in Matthew, Mark and Luke*. There is a rule when trying to trace the history of a story which says 'the simplest version is probably the oldest'. If the rule is correct in this case, then the version in the Gospel of Thomas would seem to be the most original of the four versions we have. We can therefore trace the ways in which the story was developed by the early Church.

After the first mention of the vineyard, Mark and Matthew's versions say the man 'put a fence round it, dug a hole for the wine press and built a tower'. This is a strong echo of Isaiah 5.2 and helps to identify the vineyard as 'the house of Israel and the people of Judah' (Is. 5.7).

At harvest time Matthew's version speaks of the owner first sending two *groups* of servants, who are attacked in various ways and some killed. Mark also refers to other servants after the second one, some of whom are killed – whereas Luke speaks only of three servants in all, who were treated with increasing degrees of severity but none of them actually killed. Luke's version – and Thomas' – seems simply to use a familiar device in story-telling (two or three preliminary steps and then the climax) whereas Mark and especially Matthew make the servants symbolic of the Jewish Prophets (cf the passage from Matthew 23 quoted above).

*Matthew 21.33–43; Mark 12.1–11; Luke 20.9–17.

At the first mention of the son, Mark and Luke describe him as 'the man's own dear son', thus identifying him more firmly with Jesus. (Compare accounts of the Baptism and Transfiguration, e.g. Mark 1.11 and 9.7.)

In all three of the New Testament versions the tenants throw the son out of the vineyard as well as killing him. (Matthew emphasises in his account of the crucifixion that this took place *outside* the city.)

All three also end with a question which does not occur in the Gospel of Thomas version: 'What will the owner of the vineyard do?' The answer in all three is that 'He will come and kill those men and turn the vineyard over to other tenants'. This comment must have sustained the faith of the Church a very great deal when they were being subjected to attacks by the Jewish authorities in those early years after the death of Jesus.

(One further interesting point about the three New Testament versions of this story is that at the end all three record Jesus as referring his listeners to a passage in Psalm 117 about a stone rejected by the builders being used as a corner-stone after all. The Gospel of Thomas also includes this passage about the stone, but not attached to the vineyard story.)

Having looked at the material in this chapter we should be in a better position to make a first assessment of the value of the written evidence about Jesus in the New Testament. There are four things which need to be borne in mind. First, the original material was preserved in the memories of people who had an enormous interest in it and who in any case were well used to memorising stories and poems, especially when they were presented to them in a memorisable form. Secondly, much of it was being constantly used, sometimes in worship, sometimes in debate, sometimes for instruction. Thirdly, the material was able to be 'monitored' by the surviving apostles, those companions of Jesus who had worked and lived with him during his lifetime, and had then become the leaders of those early groups of converts, seeing themselves as 'called to be witnesses' to the events of Jesus' life throughout the period we have been studying. (It is as if someone were writing now about the Second World War. Even forty years after the event there are still a large number of people about who had first-hand experience of that war and who would know the accuracy, or otherwise, of what was being written.)

But fourthly, as we have seen, it was used and *developed* to help solve new problems which the early Christians had to·face. Having given their allegiance to Jesus, they had to try to work out for themselves what they should do in circumstances which Jesus himself had not had to face and had possibly never even envisaged. The interpretations which they put on to Jesus' own words to help them in this task soon became linked firmly with the original words, and were then passed on as if they were part of the original teaching.

6

How, and why, were the gospels written?

From our study so far we have been able to discover how the stories and sayings of Jesus were preserved and circulated in the early Church. We have also learnt that there came a time when it became necessary to have *written* records alongside the oral traditions.

Though we have suggested (p. 65) the general reasons why written records were needed, it is also helpful to try to understand why each gospel in turn was written. It seems fairly likely that the same need for a written record was felt in a number of different places at roughly the same time. Because, however, the needs of each community were different and the material available to each community (or each writer) was also slightly different, the documents which emerged were by no means the same, even though three of them have a lot in common.

We do not have much clear-cut evidence about the exact purpose of each writer, but two of them did provide a brief explanation of what they were trying to do. You may remember the preface to Acts which was a major clue in identifying Luke as the author of that book. The similar preface to his gospel runs as follows:

> Many people have tried to write the story of what has happened among us; they used the reports which those who met Jesus face to face have handed down to us. I thought that I too, Your Excellency, would try to write the story down. For some time now, I have been trying to find out what actually happened, and I will put it down in its proper order. I want you to know the truth of what has been told to you. (From *New World: The Heart of the New Testament in Plain English,* by Alan T. Dale, published by OUP).

Luke speaks here of his method ('put it down in its proper order') and of his motive ('I want you to know the truth'). The other gospel in which a statement of purpose can be found also shows the writer's motive clearly enough, but the method he employed is only hinted at:

> I have not written about the many other signs which Jesus did in the presence of his friends. If I had, I should have filled the world with books! I have written as I have, to help you to see that Jesus is God's chosen Leader, God's Son – to stake your life on this fact and to live splendidly as his friend.
> (John 20.30f and 21.15, from *New World*)

The method hinted at here is the method of putting carefully selected material together to reveal a special pattern. And the writer's motive was to encourage faith in Christ among those who could see meaning in that pattern. And this is probably also the sense in which Luke was using the word 'truth'. He was not seeking simply to establish the bare facts of what happened. He was seeking to convey *through* the shaping of his material the 'truth about Jesus', a picture of Jesus which would persuade Theophilus at least to look favourably on Jesus' followers, or perhaps even to join them.

For the other two gospels in the New Testament, Mark and Matthew, we have no such introductions or epilogues. Any clue about the writer's motives or methods has to be picked up from inside the documents themselves. One can assume, however, that the purpose behind these two gospels was not very different from the purpose which Luke had in mind, even if he was writing for an individual whereas the other two were writing for whole communities. Certainly the overall shape found in Mark and Matthew was the same shape which Luke chose for his account. As a very rough guide one can say that

Mark 1	=	Matthew 3–4	=	Luke 3–4
Mark 2	=	Matthew 9	=	Luke 5
Mark 3	=	Matthew 12	=	Luke 6
Mark 4–9	=	Matthew 13–18	=	Luke 8–9
Mark 10ff	=	Matthew 19ff	=	Luke 18ff

Notice that the material in Mark appears in the same order in the other two gospels even though it is mixed in with the new material in both of them. That fact in itself is striking enough. What is even more striking is the fact that in some cases the details of the wording are very similar in all three gospels. Look for example at these three passages:

| *Mark 8.34–9.1* | *Matthew 16.24–28* | *Luke 9.23–27* |
| Then Jesus called the crowd and his disciples to him. 'If anyone wants to come with me' he told them, 'he must forget self, carry his cross and follow me. For whoever wants to save his own life will lose it, but whoever loses his life for me and for the gospel will save it. Does a person gain anything if he wins the whole world but loses his life? Of course not! There is nothing he can give to regain his life. If a person is ashamed of me and of my teaching in this godless and wicked day, then the Son of Man will be ashamed of him when he comes in the glory of his Father with the holy angels'. | Then Jesus said to his disciples: 'If anyone wants to come with me, he must forget self, carry his cross and follow me. For whoever wants to save his own life will lose it, but whoever loses his life for my sake will find it. Will a person gain anything if he wins the whole world but loses his life? Of course not! There is nothing he can give to regain his life.

For the Son of Man is about to come in the glory of his Father with his angels and then he will reward each one according to his deeds. | And he said to them all: 'If anyone wants to come with me, he must forget self, take up his cross every day and follow me. For whoever wants to save his own life will lose it, but whoever loses his life for my sake will save it. Will a person gain anything if he wins the whole world but is himself lost or defeated? Of course not!

If a person is ashamed of me and of my teaching then the Son of Man will be ashamed of him when he comes in his glory, and in the glory of the Father and of the holy angels. |

And he went on to say:
'Remember this! There
are some here who will
not die until they have
seen the Kingdom of God
come with power.'

I assure you that there
are some here who will
not die until they have
seen the Son of Man
come as King.'

I assure you that there are
some here who will
not die until they have
seen the Kingdom of God.'

The closeness of these three passages to each other can only be explained in one of two ways. Either the gospel writers copied in some way from one another, or else the oral tradition had become so fixed (at least as far as this passage is concerned) that it had remained the same even when it came to be recorded in three quite different places. Until fairly recently most people believed that Matthew and Luke had had a copy of Mark in front of them when they wrote their own gospels, but that view is perhaps not quite as widely held as it used to be. With either theory, however, (as we noted on p. 70) one has to account not only for the similarities but for the differences as well.

Those who believe that Matthew and Luke 'used' Mark argue that they changed Mark's account slightly as they went along, for one of three reasons. Either they wanted to shorten Mark's text, to make room for their own additional material, or they found Mark's style to be rather rough. (He was, after all, not a native Greek speaker. He almost certainly spoke Aramaic, like Jesus.) Or they believed his theology to be in need of modification.

Look again at the three passages quoted above. Some of the differences in Luke could certainly be changes made with the intention of shortening the passage (e.g. leaving out 'There is nothing he can give to regain his life') but if he really wanted to shorten the whole thing, why did he *add* the phrase 'every day' near the beginning? Was it perhaps that even if he were 'using' Mark, he was still very reluctant to alter the form of tradition which was found in his own church?

On the other hand the changes at the beginning and end of the passage seem to be much more deliberate. Mark suggests that Jesus addressed this passage to everyone, crowd and disciples alike. Matthew (or the tradition in Matthew's church) believed that these words were for the disciples only. This certainly makes more sense in the context in which this incident is placed. Luke's reference to 'all', on the other hand, looks like a shortened form of Mark's phrase. There are similar variations at the end. Some of these are purely stylistic, but Luke (or the tradition Luke was used to) found some difficulty in the phrase 'the Kingdom of God come with power' and so left the last bit out, while Matthew (or the tradition *he* was used to) preferred the quite different phrase 'the Son of Man come as King'.

This sort of examination of any of the parallel passages in the three gospels would reveal the same mixture of close similarities and striking differences of detail. In most cases the differences are greater than in the passages we have been studying here, but in one or two the similarities are even more complete. This is also true of a good number of passages to be found in both Matthew and Luke, but not in Mark. Once again one has to ask whether the two later writers had access to another written collection of material which they used alongside Mark, or whether they simply drew more widely on the fixed oral tradition than Mark had done.

Here is another interesting illustration of the way the gospel writers (or the earlier 'witnesses') were at one and the same time very accurate in the way they used their sources, whether they were written or oral, and yet not the least reluctant to change the shape and pattern of those sources. Look at these two passages. (There is no parallel passage in Mark).

On the Judgement Day the people of Nineveh will stand up and accuse you, because they turned from their sins when they heard Jonah preach; and there is something here, I tell you, greater than Jonah! On the Judgement Day the Queen from the South will stand up and accuse you, because she travelled halfway round the world to listen to Solomon's wise teaching; and there is something here, I tell you, greater than Solomon. When an evil spirit goes out of a man, it travels over dry country looking for a place to rest. If it can't find one it says to itself, 'I will return to my house which I left'. So it goes back and finds it empty, clean and all fixed up. Then it goes out and fetches along seven other spirits even worse than itself, and they come and live there. So that man is in worse shape, when it is all over, than he was at the beginning."

On the Judgement Day the people of Nineveh will stand up and accuse you, because they turned from their sins when they heard Jonah preach; and there is something here, I tell you, greater than Jonah! On the Judgement Day the Queen from the South will stand up and accuse the people of today, because she travelled halfway round the world to listen to Solomon's wise teaching; and there is something here, I tell you, greater than Solomon. When an evil spirit goes out of a man, it travels over dry country looking for a place to rest; if it doesn't find one, it says to itself, 'I will go back to my house which I left'. So it goes back and finds the house clean and all fixed up. Then it goes out and fetches some other spirits even worse than itself, seven of them, and they come and live there. So that man is in worse shape, when it is all over, than he was at the beginning."

Look carefully at the wording and see where you can find any differences. And then turn to a copy of Luke's gospel (11.24–32) and see whether there is such a close parallel with Matthew 12.41–45 after all?

As with the more detailed changes we examined earlier, these changes of structure and sequence which Luke in particular felt free to make could be due to a variety of reasons. Some changes may have been the result of the writer's loyalty to the tradition with which he was most familiar. Others may reflect an attempt to produce a 'more logical' sequence of material. Others again may derive from very deliberate theological reasons.

One good example of the latter is almost certainly to be found in Luke's omission of a large portion from the middle of Mark's gospel, from 6.45 to 8.26. This section contains material which has certain parallels in the previous section of Mark, i.e. 4.35–6.44, the main difference between the two sections being that the later one is set mainly in Gentile territory. Indeed some people have interpreted it as a special 'mission to Gentiles' undertaken by Jesus as a sort of interlude in his main mission to his fellow Jews. Luke, however, saw the *whole* of Jesus' work as being available to the Gentiles. So this particular device of Mark's (even if he did come across it and recognise it as such) would have been unacceptable to him.

Perhaps we can best sum up the whole process we have been trying to trace over the past few chapters in this way:

Stories told by Jesus, as well as his poems and other forms of teaching, were memorised by his disciples, as were a number of stories about him. All this material was preserved and, within careful limits, developed within the oral tradition of the early church over a period of time lasting anything between thirty and fifty years. Gradually the oral tradition gave way to written collections of material carefully selected for particular purposes. Perhaps the gospels in the New Testament were themselves the first of such documents: perhaps they in their turn were built up from earlier written collections. But either way it is clear that the writers, as we have said, were both very loyal to their sources and yet quite prepared to make changes both in detail and in structure where they believed it necessary to do so. The result of this process is a collection of four different portraits of Jesus, each one reflecting a different tradition and a different theological perspective, but together giving us a far deeper insight into the teaching of Jesus and the beliefs of the early Church about him than a single, harmonised 'biography' could possibly have done.

The 'Risen Christ', Wells Cathedral (David Wynne, 1985)

How do the gospels portray Jesus?

If you were studying a number of portraits of, say, Winston Churchill, one of the things you would probably try to do early on is to describe the outstanding features of each portrait. You could then compare the portraits to see how they differed, and also establish what they had in common despite their differences. This is the sort of process we will try to follow in looking at our four portraits of Jesus.

The first thing to notice is that the fourth gospel, John's gospel as it is called, is largely composed of long continuous blocks of material much of which takes the form of a conversation between Jesus and another individual or small group of individuals. It also seems to have been written quite a bit later. Because it is so different in character from the other three we will come to it last of all. The others are in fact often called the 'synoptic gospels' because, in contrast to John, they 'look like' each other, at least at first sight. But on closer examination certain differences, certain unique features emerge. We have already noticed that Matthew and Luke contain more material than Mark does, but there is more to the matter than that.

Let us start with Matthew, because this contains a feature which is quite unmistakeable once one has been given the necessary clue. If you look at 7.28; 11.1; 13.53; 19.1; 26.1; you will discover a refrain – 'Jesus finished saying these things, and the crowds were amazed at the way he taught' (7.28) – the same phrase appearing five times over. Almost certainly this was intended by the writer of the gospel himself as a means of dividing the document into five 'books' lying between a 'prologue' and an 'epilogue'. The 'epilogue' was the story of Jesus' Passion, a story which had its own clear traditional outline (probably settled fairly early on by reason of its frequent repetition during gatherings for worship). The 'prologue' brought together material, much of it found in no other gospel, which draws parallels between the early life of Jesus and the history of Israel (particularly the events centring on the Exodus)*. Points of comparison can be found in the mention of a Joseph, Egypt, passing through the waters (of Baptism, as of the Red Sea), a period in the wilderness before going up to the top of a mountain to receive/deliver a new law (5.1; 5.17–48). The significance of the 'five books' into which the rest of the gospel is divided can now be seen. Jesus is being portrayed by Matthew as the new Moses, bringing to the new Israel a new *Torah*, as the five-volume Jewish law-book was called.

*We saw something of this in Part I, chapter 7, where these parallels were more fully explored.

But Matthew's portrait went further than this. He saw Jesus as 'fulfilling' not only the Jewish Law, but also the Jewish prophets as well. Matthew had no doubt that Jesus was the Davidic Hero foretold by the prophets, God's Anointed One, Messiah, come to redeem his people. But the form of that redemption was the establishment of a new higher law, and a new, wider 'people of God'. This 'new Israel' with its new Torah is the Christian Church (Matthew 16.18f), an institution which embodies Jesus' teachings and shares his authority. What is more, it is an institution which is built to last. Jesus will, of course, return eventually in glory and triumph to judge the world, but that event is still some way off, and meanwhile the Church has to get on with the business of living in full accordance with the new law.

What is most striking about Luke's gospel, by contrast, is his emphasis on Jesus' concern for the Gentiles as well as for the Jews, for the outcasts of society as well as for the law-abiding. This can be seen not so much from the structure of his gospel as from the material it contains which is not found in any of the other gospels. The keynote is struck at the very beginning with the stories of Mary and Elizabeth, and with the shepherds at the stable. Other stories unique to Luke include the healing of the Roman centurion's servant and of the widow's son (ch. 7), the service offered by the women disciples (ch. 7–8), the Samaritan village (ch. 9), the parable of the Good Samaritan (ch. 10), the visit to Martha and Mary (ch. 10), the parable of the Foolish Rich Man (ch. 12), the healing of the crippled woman (ch. 13), the parable of the Prodigal Son (ch. 15), the parable of the Rich Man and Lazarus (ch. 16), the Samaritan leper (ch. 17), the parable of the Pharisee and the Tax Collector (ch. 18), and the meeting with Zacchaeus (ch. 19).

We have already noted, in the last chapter, that Luke avoided using Mark's device of indicating a 'special' Gentile mission in the middle of Jesus' ministry. As we said then, Luke saw *all* Jesus' ministry as available to the Gentiles, as it was for the downtrodden wherever they might be found, especially women and the poor. Notice too that Luke's version of the Beatitudes is much starker than Matthew's:

Matthew 5.3f, 6, 11f.	*Luke 6.20–23*
Happy are those who know they are spiritually poor: the Kingdom of Heaven belongs to them!	Happy are you poor: The Kingdom of God is yours!
Happy are those whose greatest desire is to do what God requires: God will satisfy them fully!	Happy are you who are hungry now: you will be filled!
Happy are those who mourn: God will comfort them!	Happy are you who weep now: you will laugh!
Happy are you when people insult you because a great reward is kept for you in heaven.	Happy are you when people insult you because a great reward is kept for you in heaven.
This is how the prophets who lived before you were persecuted.	For their ancestors did the very same things to the prophets.

Luke then adds four 'contra-Beatitudes' which do not appear at all in Matthew.
But how terrible for you who are rich now;
you have had your easy life!
How terrible for you who are full now;
you will go hungry!
How terrible for you who laugh now;
you will mourn and weep!
How terrible when all people speak
well of you; their ancestors said the very
same things about the false prophets.

(Luke 24–26)

When we turn to Mark it is a little more difficult to say what is distinctive about his portrait of Jesus, except in a rather negative way by showing where he differs from Matthew and Luke. So much of his material reappears in any case in the other two gospels. There does, however, seem to be a distinctive structure to his material, which was not highlighted by the other two as it did not reflect their particular concerns, even though it can be seen lying under the surface of their own very different structures.

Mark's gospel falls into two almost equal parts, divided by the events surrounding the transfiguration of Jesus in chapters 8 and 9. In the first half of the gospel Mark emphasises the miraculous deeds of Jesus. Indeed it could be thought that this section was shaped around a well-known prophecy of Isaiah:

Give strength to hands that are tired
  and to knees that tremble with
    weakness.
Tell everyone who is discouraged,
  Be strong and don't be afraid!
God is coming to your rescue,
  coming to punish your enemies.
The blind will be able to see,
  and the deaf will hear.
The lame will leap and dance,
  and those who cannot speak will
    shout for joy.

(Isaiah 35.3–6)

(Notice that in Mark 7.32, in one of the healing miracles, the deaf and dumb man is described as *mogilalos,* the precise word used in Isaiah 35.6, and a word used nowhere else in the whole of the Greek Bible.)

In this first part of the gospel there is very little teaching (especially when compared with the parallel sections of Matthew and Luke) and such teaching as there is is directed to the crowds, often in the form of 'confusing' parables. Moreover, Jesus seems to want to prevent anyone acknowledging him publicly as Messiah.

Then comes the incident on the road to Caesarea Philippi, when Jesus asks the question 'Who do people say I am?' (8.27). His disciples reply, 'Some say that you are John the Baptist: others say that you are Elijah, while others say that you are one of the prophets.' And he asked them 'What about you? Who do you say I am?' and Peter answered him 'You are the Messiah.' After this point in the story miracles become rare (though they don't disappear entirely) and emphasis is instead placed on Jesus' teaching which is now directed mostly to the disciples, trying to show them (amongst other things) how he must suffer at the hands of the authorities.

It may be that by dividing his gospel into two sections in this way, Mark was simply recording an actual change in Jesus' pattern of ministry at this point. It may be that Jesus did not wish his Messiahship to be misunderstood and so he tried to keep it secret for as long as possible, but when his closest friends at last recognised the fact, he then had to teach them what kind of Messiah he really was. On the other hand the division of the gospel in this way may be no more than a literary device intended not to reflect historical events, but to encourage a particular 'view' of Jesus, and indeed of the disciples.

Mark portrays the disciples in a very unflattering light for much of the time. Not long before the event at Caesarea Philippi, Mark records Jesus as reprimanding them pretty severely for their lack of understanding (8.17–21, see also 6.52). On two similar occasions in a boat on the lake the disciples are shown as being totally overcome by fear, and they are again reprimanded for this (4.40f; 6.50). The fact that fear interfered with their understanding is again noted (in 9.32) when they returned to Galilee for the first time after the transfiguration (see also 10.32). And then, the most surprising feature of all, the very closing event in the whole gospel is again a record of the disciples' fear and apparent lack of understanding (16.8).

It is as if Mark saw Jesus as such a figure of awe and mystery that he could only indicate the truth about him through a series of hints and clues rather than by means of a direct portrait such as Luke later attempted to produce. Perhaps he also intended his gospel to be a direct challenge to his readers. 'Are you too going to be like the first disciples, unable to understand, unable to trust the power of Jesus to save them from the midst of all their troubles? Look at all the evidence of Jesus' power. Listen to his careful teaching about the nature of God's kingdom breaking in on this world of evil and darkness. And if you still don't understand, pray that your eyes may be opened, just like the blind man at Bethsaida (8.22–26) or Bartimaeus in Jericho (11.46–52).' (We shall return to this in Chapter 9.)

There is a similar feeling of awe and mystery around the figure of Jesus as presented in the fourth gospel, that of John, and yet the mood of that gospel is quite different. We have already noted that the gospel is characterised by its long, continuous sections of conversation. It also differs from the other three in its use of geography. The other three may differ from each other in the way they divide their material up, but they have all adopted the same basic geographical framework – opening with material about Jesus in Galilee, using the so-called 'Confession of Peter' and the Transfiguration of Jesus as the end of that section, and then moving on to material linked (however loosely) with a 'journey to Jerusalem' which reaches its climax, of course, in the Passion Story.

The fourth gospel abandons that framework altogether. There is a constant movement backwards and forwards between north and south, between Galilee and Jerusalem.

For example, Jesus turns the traders out of the temple in Jerusalem, not at the end of the gospel (as in Mark) but at the very beginning (John 2). It really does look as if the author of the gospel is saying to his readers (nearly all of whom would not have had any personal knowledge or memory of the course of Jesus' life): 'The shape of the other gospels may provide an effective framework for displaying the "good news" of Jesus in a way which is easy to understand, but the real order of events was much more complex and its significance may be brought out in a different sort of way.'*

The framework adopted by John's gospel consists of a series of 'signs' (e.g. the turning of water into wine) linked with a series of symbolic statements (e.g. 'I am the bread of life') around which long discourses are woven. These discourses are obviously quite different from the single 'punch-line' sayings we were looking at in chapter 3, but they are also different from the collections of sayings which feature so noticeably in the gospels of Matthew and Luke. Those collections (for instance, the Sermon on the Mount) can very easily be analysed into the separate sayings from which they were built up, sayings which had had their own independent life within the oral tradition before they were brought

*For a further example of this, see the footnote on page 43 of Part I.

together. In John's gospel, however, the discourses seem to be more in the style of a commentary by the author on the events he has just recorded, or sometimes on events which he is just about to record.

The author's purpose, as we have already seen, was quite deliberately to build up his readers' faith in Jesus. For him the crucial question was not 'What did Jesus do?' or 'What did Jesus say?' but 'Who was this Jesus?'. What he had said and done may indeed have pointed towards the answer to this further question, but his words and actions needed to be expanded and interpreted so that his followers could come to understand the full truth about him.

Where Mark seems to have relied on challenge and shock, John's gospel sought to develop his reader's 'understanding' of Jesus through a series of profound meditations. Where Mark's emphasis was on power and conflict, John's gospel emphasises the love and spiritual peace engendered by Jesus' actions.

The differences between these four portraits are therefore pretty striking – Jesus of the New Israel; Jesus the Man for the Oppressed; Jesus the mysterious conqueror of the forces of evil; Jesus the profound teacher and bringer of peace.

It is no good, of course, saying 'Will the real Jesus stand up?' No-one whose character and nature was as complex and baffling as Jesus' was can be adequately captured even in four portraits, let alone one. Nevertheless, there must have been one view of Jesus which reflected the truth more accurately than any other, and that was Jesus' own view of himself. Is there any possibility that we can discover what this view was? It is at least worth the attempt.

8

How did Jesus see himself?

The first major problem in trying to answer this question is that, according to all four gospels, Jesus seems quite deliberately to have avoided any direct public answer to the question 'Who are you?'

One can sympathise with the irritation of the Jews who (according to John's gospel) one day gathered round him and asked, 'How long are you going to keep us in suspense? Tell us the plain truth: are you the Messiah?' (John 10.24). Their irritation must have been made even greater by the reply, 'I have already told you, but you would not believe me. The works I do by my Father's authority speak on my behalf . . . The Father and I are one.' But even though this answer avoids using the term Messiah, the central claim it makes would have been taken by the Jews to be blasphemous. They picked up stones to throw at him . . . 'You are only a man, but you are trying to make yourself God.' But that apparently was *not* what Jesus was claiming. 'How can you say that I insult God because I, chosen by the Father and sent into the world, said that I am the Son of God?' (John 10.36). The unity between God and Jesus, John's gospel seems to be explaining, was not the same as total identity between them. (Similar paradoxes occur throughout John 14–17.)

The other three gospels, and the oral tradition lying behind them, contain plenty of other examples of people calling Jesus both 'Messiah' and 'Son of God', but there (and particularly in Mark's gospel) Jesus is shown as refusing even to acknowledge the term in public (Mark 1.24, 34; 2.11) or as having to correct misunderstandings of what it meant even though he apparently accepted it in private (Mark 8.29–33).

Why should Jesus have refused to give a straight answer to this apparently simple question 'Who are you?'? Some people have suggested that it was because, in the early part of his ministry at least, Jesus was not certain in his own mind as to who he was. But none of the other actions or sayings of Jesus give the impression that he was in any way hesitant about the work he felt called to do or the message he felt called to deliver. And there are other very good reasons why Jesus should have avoided answering this question. It is often true that the simpler a question seems to be, the more complex the answer has to be, if it is not to mislead the questioner. Jesus knew full well that any straight answer to the question 'Who are you?' was bound to lead to misunderstanding.

Even if Jesus did think of himself as the 'Messiah', the 'Chosen and Anointed One' whom the Jews had been taught to believe would be sent by God to fulfil his purposes on this earth, to have used this title about himself would have begged a thousand further questions. What exactly are God's purposes? God's purposes for *whom*? As we have seen, many Jews thought God was interested in the Jewish nation alone and had no concern for the other nations at all. To them, therefore, the Messiah was a figure who would establish Jewish power over the rest of the world, even possibly exterminating all non-Jews from the face of the earth. Others may not have seen God's purposes in quite such narrow nationalistic terms, but nevertheless saw the Messiah as someone who would root out all the wicked people in the world, Jewish and non-Jewish alike. But even they saw the standard of 'good and bad' being judged in terms of the traditional Jewish Law. Unless Jesus also saw God's purposes as confined either to the Jewish race, or to the Jewish Law, he dare not identify himself publicly as Messiah – even if he saw himself as such.

And here is the big problem. *Did* he see himself as Messiah? We have seen how the early Church was convinced that Jesus was 'the one whom God has appointed judge of the living and the dead' (Acts 10.42) and yet this view of him does not seem to have been held by the disciples during his lifetime, at least not consistently. Perhaps the closest they came to it, in a warped sort of way, is reflected in the story of James and John's request to sit next to him 'in state' (Mark 10.37). Even Peter's 'confession' (Mark 8.29) seems to have been a flash-in-the-pan response rather than a dawning of a permanent new understanding. The real problem is whether this later understanding of his disciples coincided exactly with Jesus' understanding of himself, or whether they started using terms about him, like 'Judge' and 'Messiah', which he himself had refused to use.

One term which it looks very clearly as if he did use frequently, and with great significance, is 'Son of Man'. For example, according to Mark's gospel, on both occasions when the disciples spoke to him of his role as Judge-Messiah, he replied by talking not about Messiah, but about the Son of Man.

Now the odd thing about this phrase is that it occurs in as many as fifty different places in the four gospels, every time used by Jesus himself, yet it occurs only three times in the whole of the rest of the New Testament (in Acts 7.56 and twice in the Book of Revelation). Obviously, the early Church did not itself choose to use the phrase, and yet it maintained the tradition that Jesus used it constantly. But what did Jesus mean by it? It is possible that on some occasions he meant no more than 'a man' or even 'I'. Both these uses of the phrase were common in Aramaic, the language which Jesus and his followers all spoke. But on other occasions he may have been referring to a Jewish tradition, deriving from Daniel 7.13, which spoke of the Son of Man as one who would 'come with the clouds of heaven' at the time of the great judgement and to whom 'sovereignty and kingly power would be given'. But even if Jesus used 'Son of Man' as this sort of title, did he use it about himself?

The evidence is not clear. Look, for example, at Mark 8.27 and then at Matthew 16.13. Is Matthew's use of 'Son of Man' at this point simply a reflection of the Aramaic idiom referred to above, the exact equivalent of Mark's 'I'?* Certainly in places such as Mark 2.10 Jesus is obviously referring to himself. But is he at the same time alluding to the tradition derived from Daniel?

*Compare Matthew 16.15 with Mark 8.29. Compare also Matthew 5.11 with Luke 6.22, where it is Matthew that has the simple form.

Elsewhere (such as in Mark 14.62, Mark 8.38, Matthew 19.28, Matthew 16.27f) Jesus is using the phrase as the title of a supernatural being. But is he at the same time referring to himself? Not necessarily. It could in fact be argued that in, for example, Mark 8.38, Jesus is drawing a *contrast* between himself and the Son of Man; even though there is some sort of relationship between them, it is not the relationship of identity.

So where are we? Confused? Maybe, but not entirely confounded. There have been some people who have despaired of ever knowing Jesus' own mind on this particular issue – or any other issue, come to that. They have seen the beliefs of the early Church and the gospel writers as a shield, an imprenetrable shield, behind which the historical figure of Jesus has become totally hidden. But that really *is* a position of despair.

Admittedly, the difficulties in the way of reaching historical certainty are enormous. It has been compared with 'trying to work out a huge jigsaw puzzle with but the roughest idea of the picture and only one tenth of the pieces, a few of which might possibly belong to another jigsaw altogether!' But some of the pieces *are* there, and one can make *some* sensible deductions about how they relate to each other and what the complete picture is reasonably likely to be.

Whatever his exact understanding of himself in terms of 'Messiah', 'Son of Man', 'the one who is going to come' (Matthew 11.3) or whatever, it is quite clear that Jesus saw himself as one who had the almost unbearable responsibility of bringing his hearers to see that God's kingdom was about to be fully established and, what is more, that he knew the true requirements of citizenship in that kingdom. This knowledge seemed to differ in major respects from what the Jews were being led to believe on this subject by their teachers and leaders, but Jesus was more than prepared to tell these authorities how wrong they were. And behind all this lay the conviction that the 'ushering in of the new age' with all its attendant sufferings would be brought about in and through his own life and suffering.

In sum, 'Jesus thought of himself as God's human agent whose death would usher in the end of the present age', and this would, after a symbolic pause, be realised in 'the resurrection of the saints, with himself as the first-fruits'. If this is what he believed, was he completely mistaken, or have his claims been in some mysterious way fully vindicated?

Before we embark on an attempt to answer that question we need to think carefully about the place of evidence in trying to reach any conclusions where claims of 'miracle' are involved – and such claims are involved in this case. It is sometimes suggested that in any situation where 'miracle' is being claimed, 'evidence' is not needed, merely 'faith'. Faith does, of course, enter into this matter. If your view of the world is one which has absolutely no room for the possibility of 'miracle' (however that may be defined), then no amount of 'evidence' will be able to persuade you that 'the impossible' has occurred. On the other hand, if you believe that 'normal' human experience does not itself necessarily define the limits of what *could* happen, then the idea of 'miracle' is not ruled out altogether. Even so, the more abnormal any event may be which someone claims to have happened, the greater is the need for supporting evidence, otherwise faith soon becomes simple gullibility.

An important example of the point under discussion here is found in the story of Jesus' 'virgin birth'. In 'assessing the evidence' for the truth of this claim it should be noted that Paul, who gives us the earliest written account of the ministry of Jesus (his letters, as we have already seen, were written some years before the first of the Gospels), says nothing at all about Jesus being born of a virgin – nor is there any such claim in the Acts of the Apostles, despite the many 'accounts of Jesus' contained in that book. The only two passages in the whole of the New Testament which make any reference to it at all are the 'infancy narratives' in Matthew and Luke, and you will remember that we have already noted (Part I. p. 31) that in these narratives 'history, story, symbol, legend, prophecy and poetry are all intertwined' and that 'we have to read these stories not as straightforward recordings of what actually happened, but as attempts to demonstrate what an extraordinary and significant person Jesus was'.

There are in fact two quite separate issues bound up in any discussion of whether stories of a 'virgin birth' (or, to be more accurate, a virginal conception) are true or not. One is the 'historical' question of whether the evidence is strong enough to indicate that the events 'actually happened' as described by Matthew and Luke. The other is the 'theological' question of whether the claims made about Jesus by his disciples would *require* that he was conceived by a direct act of God. On this second question theologians disagree even today. Some argue that he could not have been 'properly' human if he did not have a human father; others argue that if he did have a human father, then Paul's claim that 'God was in Christ reconciling the world to himself' (II Cor. 5.19) cannot have been true.

This is not the place to try to argue through the theological question. It must be enough to note that there are valid theological reasons on both sides of the argument. (See, for example, *The Nature of Christian Belief* (CHP 1986) paras 56–61.)* As for the historical question, the crucial point must be that neither Paul nor (apparently) any of the disciples who preached in Jerusalem in the first few years after Jesus' death knew anything of such a tradition. If they *had* known, they would surely have used it as further proof of their claims about Jesus.

The historian of today will therefore be very hesitant about claiming that there is sufficient historical evidence to *prove* that Jesus was 'born of the Virgin Mary'. But of course the silence of Paul and the other disciples does not in turn *prove* that things didn't happen that way, it merely indicates that they were unaware of such a claim ever having been made. So even if it would be unwise to argue that Jesus must have been the Son of God because we 'know' he was miraculously conceived, it is not impossible to argue that he must have been miraculously conceived because we are convinced (on other grounds) that he was the Son of God.

We have here entered on a type of argument where we must be very clear what we are doing. We must know what *sort* of questions we are asking before we try to answer them. This warning applies, as we have already suggested, not only to discussions about who Jesus was, but also to discussions about whether his beliefs about himself were in the end vindicated.

In the final chapter of this book we will look at some of the 'theological' questions which are central to this discussion. But first we need to clarify some of the 'historical' questions. And so we need to look very closely at all the evidence which we can find for the claim that Jesus overcame death in the way he predicted he would. We have seen already that the works of Josephus, as they have been handed down to us, contain some reference to Jesus' resurrection, however uncertain the authority or significance of that passage may be. But we obviously need to look once again at the written evidence of the New Testament itself and try to assess the historical value we can place on that.

*Quoted, in part, in the Authors' Postlude at the end of this book.

9

What happened at the Resurrection?

The earliest *written* evidence about the Resurrection comes from Paul's first letter to the Corinthians (though it is mentioned in general terms in the very earliest of all Paul's letters, the first one to the Thessalonians). Paul reminded the Corinthians (as we saw in Part II, chapter 4) that when he had visited them a few months/years earlier he had 'passed onto them what he had received': 'that Christ died for our sins, as written in the Scriptures; that he was buried and that he was raised to life three days later, as written in the Scriptures; that he appeared to Peter and then to all twelve apostles. Then he appeared to more than five hundred of his followers at once, most of whom are still alive, although some have died. Then he appeared to James, and afterwards to all the apostles. Last of all he appeared also to me – . . .'.

You will notice immediately that Paul does not say what the 'appearances' were like, nor when they happened, nor over what period of time.

You may also notice that Paul's account matches the accounts given elsewhere in the New Testament only in the first two events, namely the appearances 'to Peter and to the Twelve'.

It is only natural to try to match up the different accounts in the New Testament in the way we have just suggested you might do. But it can sometimes be very misleading to attempt this, particularly if it leads us to mix together material which was intended to be seen separately. This is especially true of the four gospel accounts. It is very important to remember that when each gospel was written it was written for a particular church or for a particular individual. Very few churches, if any, in the early days would have had more than one gospel in its possession. The resurrection story in each gospel (at least in each of the synoptic gospels) was intended to be understood as being complete in itself.

This is, at first sight, a most surprising remark to make about Mark's gospel, which appears to have very little to say about the resurrection at all, apart from the discovery that Jesus' tomb was empty, and what little it does say ends with the words 'So they went out and ran from the tomb, distressed and terrified. They said nothing to anyone, because they were afraid.' This is the final sentence in the most reliable of the ancient manuscripts containing Mark's gospel. But it is such a strange way to end a book which claims to contain 'the Good

News about Jesus Christ, the Son of God' (Mark 1.1) that various early Christians provided various additional verses in an attempt to make the gospel end in a more expected way, and some of these verses were included in most 'official' translations of St Mark until fairly recently. And it is of course true that when Matthew and Luke came to 'develop' Mark's gospel in their different ways they both added further material which enabled their gospels to end on a note of definite joy, rather than a note of apparent fear.

But there are, as we said in Part II chapter 7, good reasons why Mark may have wanted to end his gospel the way he did. In the early part of his account of Jesus he had stressed Jesus' use of parable, and the way in which the disciples had been challenged to reach towards an understanding of the truth, rather than having it simply 'told' to them. Mark's readers were being challenged in the same sort of way because, Mark believed, that was the only way in which a real grasp of the truth could be achieved. Moreover, the key to this final scene of his gospel (the 'big hint' he wanted his readers to respond to) was the remark of the young man who spoke to the women at the tomb: 'Now go and give this message to his disciples, including Peter: "He is going to Galilee ahead of you; there you will see him, just as he told you." ' Galilee: that is the clue. *Galilee*, where he had performed virtually all his miracles; where Mark tells us, he had defied 'the laws of nature' by walking across the surface of the Lake Tiberias, had shown his control over 'the forces of nature' by quelling a storm, and had finally been 'transfigured' in the presence of a select group of disciples – and on each of these occasions the disciples had been totally overcome with fear and astonishment. The end of Mark's gospel is therefore all of a piece with the earlier part, and his readers are being challenged to 'see' Jesus (even after he had been put to death) as they had already come to 'see' him in Galilee.

Matthew's account of the Resurrection is much more explicit and contains some additional and important material. First of all he adds a couple of episodes which counter the argument that Jesus' tomb could have been empty because his disciples had stolen the body (see Matthew 27.62–66 and 28.11–15). Secondly he adds more drama to some of Mark's detail: for example, the 'young man' is directly identified as an 'angel', and the moving of the stone from the mouth of the tomb is accompanied by an earthquake. Thirdly, Jesus himself appears and is seen by the women. They, you will notice, are described as 'afraid, yet filled with joy' and Jesus on meeting them also tells them not to be afraid. All of this material which Matthew has used alters the mood of his gospel account compared with Mark's. Where in Mark the women are filled with fear, here they are 'filled with joy'; where in Mark there is no mention of the risen body of Jesus, here Jesus himself appears. The resurrection may still be mysterious but it is also the clear beginning of a triumphant new age when the whole earth will hear the gospel.

But you will notice, on reading Matthew's account, that he also expands the references to 'Galilee'. The women are told twice, once by the angel, and once by the risen Jesus, that the disciples must go to Galilee. The story continues: 'The eleven disciples went to the hill in Galilee where Jesus had told them to go. When they saw him they worshipped him, even though some of them doubted. Jesus drew near and said to them, "I have been given all authority in heaven and on earth. Go, then, to all peoples everywhere and make them my disciples: baptise them in the name of the Father, Son and the Holy Spirit, and teach them to obey everything I have commanded you. And I will be with you always, to the end of the age." ' It is at this point that Matthew ends his gospel. The story as it stands has probably been heavily influenced by the traditions of the early Church (the words used in the rite of Baptism in the Church sound a little strange on the lips of Jesus at this point) but Matthew certainly follows up in his own way the 'big hint' about Galilee which we find in Mark's closing verses.

Luke, on the other hand, not merely ignores Mark's reference to Galilee, but actually turns it on its head. The women at the tomb are met by two men, in dazzling garments, who ask, 'Why are you looking among the dead for one who is alive? He is not here; he has been raised. Remember what he said to you while he was in Galilee: "The Son of Man must be handed over to sinful men, be crucified, and three days later rise to life." ' From then on Luke's version makes everything happen in Jerusalem and the immediate vicinity. In fact the disciples are explicitly forbidden to leave Jerusalem. (This might possibly be explained by Luke's apparent interest in stressing the unity of the early Church, with Jerusalem as its centre of government – a model which would presumably have appealed very strongly to Theophilus, who must have been an admirer of the strength and unity of Rome itself.)

There are some other details in Luke's account which are also worth some attention. The women who met the risen Jesus are identified as being well known among his followers. 'The women were Mary Magdalene, Joanna, and Mary the mother of James; they and the other women with them told these things to the apostles. But the apostles thought that what the women said was nonsense, and they did not believe them.' According to some manuscripts of Luke's gospel, 'Peter got up and ran to the tomb; he bent down and saw the linen wrappings but nothing else. Then he went back home amazed at what had happened.' (Neither in Mark nor Matthew is it said that Peter also witnessed the empty tomb.) Certainly Luke records that the Risen Jesus actually appeared to Peter face to face somewhat later on (24.34). (See also I Corinthians 15.5.)

Luke also records at some length another incident which neither Mark nor Matthew mention in any way:
On that same day two of Jesus' followers were going to a village named Emmaus, about eleven kilometres from Jerusalem, and they were talking to each other about all the things that had happened. As they talked and discussed, Jesus himself drew near and walked along with them; they saw him, but somehow did not recognise him. Jesus said to him, 'What are you talking about to each other, as you walk along?'

They stood still with sad faces. One of them, named Cleopas, asked him, 'Are you the only visitor in Jerusalem who doesn't know the things that have been happening there these last few days?' 'What things?' he asked.

'The things that happened to Jesus of Nazareth,' they answered. 'This man was a prophet and was considered by God and by all the people to be powerful in everything he said and did. Our chief priests and rulers handed him over to be sentenced to death, and he was crucified. And we had hoped that he was to be the one who was going to set Israel free! Besides all that, this is now the third day since it happened. Some of the women of our group surprised us; they went at dawn to the tomb, but could not find his body. They came back saying they had seen a vision of angels who told them that he is alive. Some of our group went to the tomb and found it exactly as the women had said, but they did not see him.'

Then Jesus said to them, 'How foolish you are, how slow you are to believe everything the prophets said! Was it not necessary for the Messiah to suffer these things and then enter his glory?' And Jesus explained to them what was said about himself in all the Scriptures, beginning with the books of Moses and the writings of all the prophets.

As they came near to the village to which they were going, Jesus acted as if he were going further; but they held him back, saying, 'Stay with us; the day is almost over and it is getting dark.' So he went in to stay with them. He sat down to eat with them, took the bread, and said the blessing; then he broke the bread and gave it to them. Then their eyes were opened and they recognised him, but he disappeared from their sight. They said to each other, 'Wasn't it like a fire burning in us when he talked to us on the road and explained the Scriptures to us?'

They got up at once and went back to Jerusalem, where they found the eleven disciples gathered together with the others and saying, 'The Lord is risen indeed! He has appeared to Simon!'

The two then explained to them what had happened on the road, and how they had recognised the Lord when he broke the bread.   (Luke 24.13–35)

There are several features of this story which are worth noting. First, the resurrection body of Jesus, according to Luke, seemed not to be bound by normal laws of time and space: secondly, through Jesus' teaching about the scriptures the followers came to see that their original understanding of what the Messiah would be like was wrong; and thirdly, it was in the breaking of the bread that the followers suddenly recognized him. It was as though this meal was a reminder to them of past meals shared with Jesus and a foretaste of the eucharistic meals of the church (when Jesus' words and actions at the Last Supper were re-presented), in which they also 'knew' his risen presence.

The theme of sharing a meal with Jesus continues in the story which immediately follows:

While the two were telling them this, suddenly the Lord himself stood among them and said to them, 'Peace be with you.' They were terrified, thinking that they were seeing a ghost. But he said to them, 'Why are you alarmed? Why are these doubts coming up in your minds? Look at my hands and feet, and see that it is I myself. Feel me, and you will know, for a ghost doesn't have flesh and bones, as you can see I have.'

He said this and showed them his hands and his feet. They still could not believe, they were so full of joy and wonder; so he asked them, 'Have you anything here to eat?' They gave him a piece of cooked fish, which he took and ate in their presence.

Then he said to them, 'These are the very things I told you about while I was still with you; everything written about me in the Law of Moses, the writings of the prophets, and the Psalms had to come true.'

Then he opened their minds to understand the Scriptures, and said to them, 'This is what is written: the Messiah must suffer and must rise from death three days later, and in his name the message about repentance and the forgiveness of sins must be preached to all nations, beginning in Jerusalem. You are witnesses of these things. And I myself will send upon you what my Father has promised. But you must wait in the city until the power from above comes down upon you'.   (Luke 24.36–49)

Luke seems to be at some pains to point out the close continuation between Jesus' resurrection body and his earthly body. It may be that this was because he wanted to be faithful to his original sources. He had received a tradition of Jesus eating and drinking with his disciples after his resurrection (see Acts 10.36–43). Or it may have been his way of countering an idea which some people were propagating towards the end of the first century that there was a real separation between the human and the spiritual body of Jesus. The divine

Christ, according to this theory (which is technically known as the Docetic heresy), descended upon Jesus at his baptism and returned to heaven before the crucifixion. In other words Jesus' human body was only a kind of 'pretend' body. Luke wanted to say that the 'human' and the 'risen' body of Jesus were one and the same – hence his emphasis upon the wounds, and upon Jesus eating a meal with his disciples after the Resurrection.

He also includes another short incident which neither Mark nor Matthew mention. Luke writes: 'Then he led them out of the city as far as Bethany, where he raised his hands and blessed them. As he was blessing them, he departed from them and was taken up into heaven.' This fairly brief, and rather obscure, reference is filled out considerably in the opening section of the Acts of the Apostles, though the existence of two (or is it three?) accounts of Jesus' 'parting from them' cannot be very easily reconciled one with another (see Luke 24.50–52, Acts 1.2 and Acts 1.9). But these internal discrepancies within Luke's own writings are not as significant or as surprising as the fact that Luke is the only one of the four evangelists who makes any mention at all of an 'ascension' as such.* Perhaps Luke, who was particularly familiar with Paul's claim that the 'risen Christ' had appeared to him (near Damascus), wanted for some reason to indicate that that 'appearance' was of a different character from the appearances to the Twelve. An 'ascension' provided a clear demarcation between those appearances closely associated with the resurrection and those which were both later and in other parts of the country.

In John's gospel the resurrection stories have echoes (perhaps conscious echoes, though *only* echoes) of all the other gospels. They seem, however, to have a special link with Luke's account. In John it is only one woman, Mary of Magdala, who goes to the tomb. There is no mention of guards, young men, nor (at first) of angels. Mary runs straight back to the disciples and her story brings Peter and another of the Twelve running to the tomb. (Contrast the initial scepticism of the disciples as recorded by Luke.) After Peter and the other disciple have gone Mary does see two angels, and then meets Jesus himself. She does not realise who it is and recognises him only when he speaks her name.

Then John records an appearance to the disciples 'behind locked doors' in Jerusalem. This has certain parallels with Luke's account of Jesus' appearance in Jerusalem, but John splits the incident into two separate appearances, a full week apart. In fact it might be more true to say that John splits the incident into *three* appearances, the last of which occurred 'some time later . . . by the Sea of Tiberias'. According to John, this third occasion was the one on which Jesus ate fish and bread with them. It is almost as if John were saying, 'Luke condensed the story too much; this is how it really happened.' Even more strikingly John makes no reference, as Luke had done, either to an 'ascension' or to a later 'coming of the Spirit'. In John's account it was during the first appearance in Jerusalem that Jesus 'breathed on them, saying "Receive the Holy Spirit".'

It is clear, then, that each of the four gospels gives a very different account of what happened after the empty tomb had been discovered. (There are other differences besides the ones noted above.) All four do agree, however, on two things. *First*, they all claim with absolute assurance that Jesus' tomb was empty (empty of a body, that is; John speaks of the wrappings which had been round the body still lying there, and the account in the other three does not rule that possibility out). *Secondly*, all four are agreed (strongly hinted at by Mark,

*There is one exception, the very ambiguous reference to 'ascending' in John 20.17 – which uses a quite different Greek word from any of the ones used by Luke.

clearly affirmed by the other three) that Jesus rejoined their fellowship after his death, and promised them his continuing presence with them as they went out into the world to bear witness to what had happened.

Of course various explanations of the empty tomb can be (and indeed have been) put forward – that the women had mistaken the tomb in the early light; that the body had been stolen by Jesus' opponents; that Jesus had not in fact been dead when he was taken down from the cross and had simply revived in the tomb and walked out. However, quite apart from the difficulties implicit in any of these 'explanations' there is the over-riding objection that if Jesus, alive or dead, were known to be still in Jerusalem when stories of his resurrection started up, it would have been easy for his enemies to produce the body (or to produce witnesses who had seen him subsequently alive) and so refute the stories immediately. This simply did not happen.

There are two remaining possibilities. One is that someone sympathetic to Jesus stole the body and then was too frightened (or too devious) to admit to what he had done. If that were indeed what happened, then every single one of the resurrection appearances must have been a delusion with no underlying physical or even spiritual reality, and the central core of the early Church's 'gospel' was (consciously or unconsciously) an empty mockery, however valuable the moral teaching associated with it may have been.

The other possibility is that the witness of the gospels is true. Something literally extra-ordinary happened to Jesus' body and the power which had been so characteristic of his life re-asserted itself despite his death.

Faced with these two possibilities, how can we decide between them and be sure that we have found the truth of the matter? It is, of course, not often possible to be absolutely *sure* of the truth when dealing with events from the past, even ordinary everyday events. With an event of this magnitude it becomes even more difficult than usual to establish certainty. But equally with an event of this magnitude it becomes far more important than usual to try to decide which way the evidence is pointing.

Our examination of the Gospel material has left us with two possibilities, one positive and one negative, either of which would apparently fit the historical evidence so far. But there is one more piece of evidence we must take into account, and that is the very existence of the early Church. Before reaching any verdict on this question we must give full weight to the fact that Jesus' friends and disciples were convinced that he had risen from the dead and had re-entered into fellowship with them. As a result they were turned from a collection of frightened disillusioned individuals into a band of confident 'witnesses' whose joyous enthusiasm was so infectious that it swept thousands of converts into their company within a few weeks, and sustained them through wave after wave of hostility and persecution by the Jewish and Roman authorities.

Which is more likely – that this joy, enthusiasm and steadfastness was built on a delusion, or that it was built on the truth, however extraordinary that truth might be?

10

The question of Jesus

In the opening pages of this book the claim was made that 'a man who has had such an influence upon the world must be worth getting to know.' This claim was later developed in the following passage: 'People still find themselves challenged to make up their minds about him. When you are trying to find the answer to a problem, you often have to ask a lot of questions to help you "make up your mind". In this book we try to set out the questions to which you need to find answers when trying to make up your mind about Jesus. We have also tried to show the sort of evidence which is available to help you find those answers. Most of the questions, and therefore most of the evidence, could be described as "historical", but there comes a point at which the question of Jesus ceases to be simply the sort of question which a historian could be expected to answer.'

That point has now been reached. The questions 'Did Jesus rise from the dead?' and 'Did his death usher in the new age, the Kingdom of God?' are not open to the same sort of answer you could give to questions such as 'Did Jesus ever visit Jerusalem?' or 'Did his teaching have any impact on the Pharisees?' They are not straightforward 'historical' questions, requiring simply a historian's judgement based on historical evidence. They are questions of a different kind. They are questions which challenge us at the deepest level to think about what we ourselves believe. And they cannot be answered by reason and intelligence alone. They demand commitment as well as careful judgement (*'as well as'*, not 'instead of', please note!). To answer 'yes' to the question: 'Did Jesus rise from the dead?' has all kinds of implications. It commits one to the view that there is more to human existence than the material world of space and time. It further commits one to the belief that space can give way to infinity, that the eternal can break into (and co-exist with) time. In short, it is an acceptance of God's existence and of his activity in the world of which we are part.

No wonder that Mark felt that he could give his readers no more than hints and pointers to what happened at the resurrection. Even though the final message of the gospel was 'He is going to Galilee ahead of you: there you will see him, just as he told you', the new fellowship to which this was pointing was not simply the old fellowship renewed after a brief interruption. It was a *fulfilment* of that earlier fellowship. It was a fellowship of a stronger and stranger kind.

And it is here that the real importance of Jesus lies. The fellowship which the early disciples experienced with the risen Jesus was not just an odd, one-off phenomenon. It is an experience which has subsequently been shared by millions of Christian disciples down the ages. Jesus has indeed 'changed the world', not only by his teaching but by the challenge which he brought to the world through the experience of his first disciples. Whatever picture of human life people have built up from their investigations and enquiries into the world around them, the experience of Jesus' disciples (both before and after his death) has stood as a challenge to the completeness of that picture. It faces men with the question: 'Is your picture of human life big enough to accommodate the experience to which those disciples bore witness?'

It is often said that Jesus 'revealed God to men', but we must be very careful how we use that phrase. It cannot mean that Jesus' teaching (or the experience of his first disciples) was so clear-cut and unambiguous that all our questions about God are answered, that now we know and understand all that there is to be known and understood. To claim this is to misunderstand both the nature of the issues involved and the nature of Jesus' teaching.

To grasp in any adequate way the relationship between created and uncreated, between God and man, demands the exercise of faith as well as reason, of will as well as intellect. Jesus therefore did not spend a great deal of time instructing his disciples. He sought instead to challenge them into a response. And through their record of their experience with him, the New Testament, he continues to challenge succeeding generations including our own. It is only in this sense, and only by this method, that he 'reveals' God to us.

It is not surprising, then, that the further we go in our study of Jesus the greater the number of questions which seem to arise and the fewer the answers which can simply be presented to us ready-made. Jesus' challenge to us is not to turn to other people for answers but to listen to his questions and work out our own answers – and to commit ourselves to those answers at the same time.

The focus of Jesus' challenge, the central question to which the gospel writers draw our special attention, is the question he put to his disciples at Caesarea Philippi: 'Who do people say I am? What about you? Who do *you* say I am?'

But the full significance of that question appears only when we remember that Jesus believed himself to be 'God's agent' on earth, and that after his death his disciples also came to claim that 'God was acting in him'. The final challenge that confronts us from the New Testament is therefore this:

God in Christ asks 'Who am I?' and waits for us to reply.

Authors' Postlude

The English poet Samuel Taylor Coleridge used to say that it was only when you approached the Bible as if it were just like any other book that you came to realise its true nature in all its uniqueness. He was making this point in the face of those (the great majority of people) who held that because the Bible was 'the word of God' it had to be read and studied in a way quite different from all other documents. That view (though far less widespread) still exists today, and those who hold it could well find themselves disturbed by some of the material in the following pages – because these pages were written with Coleridge's words very much in mind.

To be able to explore the uniqueness of the New Testament by approaching it 'as if it were just like any other book', two main assumptions have to be made. You have to be prepared to use all the available tools and techniques of the historian, and this in turn means that you have to approach the central character, Jesus of Nazareth, 'as if he were just like any other man' – at least in the first instance.

On the first point it might be useful to quote from the statement by the House of Bishops on *The Nature of Christian Belief* (CHP 1986). In the section entitled *Faith and History* they write as follows:

> The Church has no short-cut private road to historical certainty. On any view of scriptural inspiration it is important for questions to be asked about historical statements . . . Historical fact does matter . . . (and it) would be wrong . . . to neglect all historical investigation . . . But once such enquiry is allowed, it has to be free . . . The Church has nothing to lose but everything to gain from the responsible pursuit of historical criticism (paras 22, 27 and – mainly – 28).

'Responsible historical criticism' will involve not only the responsible use of the historian's techniques, but also the adoption of the historian's basic approach, which is an essentially scientific approach. This means that the writer will present the evidence (at least in the first instance) without any of the presuppositions of faith.

This (as we have suggested) has particular implications for the presentation of the person of Jesus. A historical approach has to present him, and try to understand him, in strictly human terms. For some readers this may be an unfamiliar experience, but (as with the Bible itself) Coleridge's words will almost certainly prove to be true about Jesus as well: it is only when you approach him in these fully human terms, that you come to realise his true nature in all its uniqueness.

It is in this context that the particularly difficult question of Jesus' Virginal Conception must be set. The matter is dealt with directly on pp 89-90, but it may be helpful when reading that passage to bear in mind the following quotations from *The Nature of Christian Belief:*

... we are confronted here with an issue to which both the reasoned assessment of biblical evidence and the theological convictions of faith are proper responses. On both grounds arguments have been advanced both for and against regarding the Virginal Conception as historically factual ... (para 52).

... it is important to remember the understanding of human reproduction in the ancient world. The mother was thought of simply as a vessel to contain and feed the child. It was the father alone who contributed all the human material that would develop into the future person. To affirm creation by the Holy Spirit, with no human father ... is therefore to affirm a completely new beginning, a human person without biological ancestry ... (para 59).

... Jesus' Sonship in relation to God the Father is of a unique character, distinct in kind from the adoptive relationship we receive through him ... At the same time it is essential that he should be truly and fully human ... It is this need to insist on the completeness and authenticity of Christ's humanity which has led some Christian thinkers in modern times to question whether ... any human being created by such a divine act could be authentically one with us in our full humanity ... The Virginal Conception, on this view, is the Church's historically chosen symbol for the belief that ... the birth of Jesus Christ marked ... a unique act of God for redeeming and fulfilling the world ... (para 60).

The central miracle, the heart of the Christian understanding of God, is the Incarnation itself. It is the faith of us all that this is truly expressed in the affirmation of the catholic Creeds that in Jesus Christ, fully God and fully human, the Second Person of the Blessed Trinity is incarnate. (There are) divergences between Christian scholars on the relation of the Virginal Conception of Our Lord to this great mystery, and on the question whether or not that conception is to be regarded as historical fact as well as imagery symbolic of divine truth ... But all of us accept: first, that the belief that Our Lord was conceived in the womb of Mary by the creative power of God the Holy Spirit without the intervention of a human father can be held with full intellectual integrity; secondly, that only this belief, enshrined in the Creeds, can claim to be the teaching of the universal Church ... expressing the faith ... that in Christ God has taken the initiative for our salvation by uniting our human nature with himself, so bringing into being a new humanity (para 62).

The pages that follow claim at least to be consistent with that statement, even if they do not contain a full and explicit exposition of all the theology within it. They offer, if you like, proto-theology rather than theology itself. But it is the belief of the editors (as it was of Alan Dale himself) that one's final amalgam of faith and understanding is built by stages, and does not spring fully grown from one's first encounter with the gospels. At each stage, however, that encounter with the gospels needs to be experienced as a challenge, not just as an academic exercise. It is our hope that this exploration of 'the question of Jesus' which we present here will enable just such an experience to occur.

Colin Alves
Christopher Herbert

Notes about the illustrations

'The Good Shepherd' For the first 200 or so years of the Christian religion there were no attempts to portray Jesus in paint or sculpture; the influence of the Jewish law which forbade the making of images was still strong. As the religion spread westwards through the Roman empire, however, paintings appeared on Christian tombs and statues were placed in houses in the same way that Roman citizens commemorated their gods. This statue dates from about AD330. Its subject was popular not only because Jesus had described himself as the Good Shepherd, but for two other reasons: a strong but beardless youth represented the 'ideal man' of Greek and Roman taste; a very similar statue of Hermes the Ram-carrier could often be found in pagan households – Christians who were in danger of persecution could safely put a symbol of their faith on view without its being recognised as such.

'Christ the Ruler of All' As outlying eastern parts of the Roman Empire also became Christian, people began to turn to the idea of a powerful eastern king, bearded and majestic, rather than the young Greek hero, as a more 'appropriate' way to picture Jesus. From this way of depicting him in art comes the tradition of 'ikons': holy pictures, painted with prayer and reverence, which can still be seen today in the homes and churches of Orthodox Christians. Our photograph shows a mosaic of almost frightening strength, made shortly before AD1100 for the Greek church of Daphni. Jesus is seen as the judge and ruler of all the world.

'Christ Mocked' During the early Middle Ages, while the eastern Church continued to picture Jesus in formalised style as Ruler and Lord, in western Europe painters began to show him as a living, suffering human being. (This change was at least partly brought about by the enormously influential preaching of St Francis, who taught of Jesus in this way.) Pictures from the Middle Ages often show incidents from Jesus' life, sometimes realistically, sometimes using symbols which were easier for people to understand then than they are now. Hieronymus Bosch (1450-1516), a Flemish painter, is best known for some amazing fantasy pictures which have inspired many an SF book cover, but when he painted 'Christ Mocked' he had a serious point to make. In the Bible story Jesus was mocked by Roman soldiers, but the gentle Christ of this picture is accepting pain and blows from people of all kinds: some brutal, some malicious, some just ordinary and uncaring.

The Tapestry, Coventry Cathedral The rest of the photographs in this book are of works of art from our own times, the years after the Second World War. After that war Coventry Cathedral, which had been destroyed by bombs, was rebuilt and the painter Graham Sutherland (1903-80) asked to design a huge tapestry which would hang behind the high altar. Completed in 1957, this shows Jesus again as the Risen Lord; around him as the traditional emblems of the four gospel-writers: a man for Matthew, a lion for Mark, an ox for Luke and an eagle for John. Between the feet of Jesus – untraditionally – stands the tiny figure of a human being, upright beneath the mushroom-cloud curves of the white robe.

Crucifixion, Birmingham Cathedral Modern sculpture in the western world has been much influenced by the art of Africa and the Pacific islands. You may feel that there are echoes of such influence in the figure of Jesus on the cross made in 1983 for Birmingham Cathedral by Peter Eugene Ball. This spare, powerful carving is shaped from driftwood, embellished with copper and gold-leaf.

The 'Risen Christ', west front of Wells Cathedral The west front of Wells Cathedral was carved 600 years ago with some 297 stone figures; dominating them all should have been the Risen Christ in the topmost niche, but most of that statue fell long ago, leaving only the section from the knees down, with no record of how it looked when complete. Being asked, in 1983, to fill that niche was a tough commission for sculptor David Wynne: he had to respect the existing figures, yet produce something more than an imitation, something of his own time and feeling. The result, unveiled in 1985, shows Jesus with one hand raised in a gesture of blessing, the other reaching out to the world.

Acknowledgements

The authors would like to acknowledge with gratitude the contribution which the Rt. Rev. John Tinsley, former Bishop of Bristol, made to their thinking, particularly as regards the last chapter of this book.

Unless otherwise stated, all Scripture quotations are from the Good News Bible (British usage edition) published by The Bible Societies and Collins. Old Testament©American Bible Society 1976, New Testament © American Bible Society 1966, 1971, 1976. Used by permission.

Photographs are reproduced by kind permission of the following:
'The Good Shepherd': The Mansell Collection.
'Christ the Ruler of All' (Christos Pantokrator): Michael Holford.
'Christ Mocked' by Hieronymus Bosch: The Trustees of The National Gallery, London.
The Tapestry, Coventry Cathedral: The Education Officer, Coventry Cathedral.
Crucifixion, Birmingham Cathedral: Peter Eugene Ball.
The 'Risen Christ', Wells Cathedral: Channel Four Television.

Passages from *New World: the Heart of the New Testament in Plain English* (OUP) are reproduced by kind permission of Oxford University Press.